MANY GIFTS
ONE LORD

Jordan,

May the hord fill you richly
with His Spirit and reveal
His specific gifts for you!

Pastor Healey

MANY GIFTS
ONE LORD

*A Biblical Understanding of the Variety
of Spiritual Gifts among Early Christians
and in the Church Today*

HARLEY H. SCHMITT

Cover design: Lecy Design
Text design by James F. Brisson

Xulon Press
11350 Random Hills Road
Suite 800
Fairfax, VA 22030
www.xulonpress.com

CONTENTS

ACKNOWLEDGMENTS

Many people offered support through prayer, suggestions, and encouragement which aided in the writing of this volume. First, I want to express my appreciation to my wife, Beverly, and my children who supported me during the many days and weeks over the years that I spent away from them in either research or teaching what I had researched. I also want to acknowledge the many faithful members of Brooklyn Park Lutheran Church who have allowed me to make mistakes. I especially want to acknowledge Jim Kersting, a friend and member of Brooklyn Park Lutheran, for his faithfulness in reading and editing. I also desire to express my sincere appreciation to seminary professors Dr. Mark Hillmer, the late Dr. Lowell Satre, and Dr. Arland Hultgren for suggestions, guidance, and encouragement.

I also want to express my appreciation to former Minnesota Governor, Al Quie, and to Larry Christenson and the late Dr. Dennis Pederson for their encouragement to submit the manuscript for publication.

Finally, but most of all, I give praise and thanks to the Lord for graciously working in my life, allowing me to experience his grace in a new and special way each day. I praise him for guiding me and sustaining me at times when I felt like quitting. To him be all praise and glory.

INTRODUCTION

"If you were charged with being a Christian, would there be enough evidence to convict you?" Such a question leads us to do some soul searching as it relates to our Christian life and commitment. We could also rephrase that question, "If you have noticed an increasing emptiness in your life, would the evidence in the lives of the Christians you meet attract you to Jesus?"

In most other areas of life, recognizable results catch our attention. We may ask, "Is there some visible demonstration that what these Christians are proclaiming is true?" "Is there any evidence that their message is effective?" So we also need to ask ourselves, "Is there enough activity within the Christian church to even attract attention?"

We are impressed and intrigued as we read of miraculous incidents in the Bible that took place through the power of the Spirit of God. Those thus empowered had an unusual ability to accomplish and perform the impossible. In the early life of the Christian church there was a close correlation between what was proclaimed and what was accomplished. We can understand why many were attracted to the Christian faith because there was evidence that they were empowered by God. The message the Christians taught was not simply words that never became a reality; it was a message accented with a demonstration of its authenticity.

When we think of what the early Christians were able to do through the work of God's Spirit, we wonder what might be possible today. These passages give us some help:

> Very truly, I tell you, the one who believes in me will also do the works that I do and, in fact, will do greater works than these, because I am going to the Father. I will do whatever you ask in my name, so that the Father may be glorified in the Son. If in my name you ask me for anything, I will do it (JOHN 14:12-13).

Ask, and it will be given you; search, and you will find;
knock, and the door will be opened for you. For everyone who
asks receives, and everyone who searches finds, and for
everyone who knocks, the door will be opened (MATT. 7:7-8).

But you will receive power when the Holy Spirit has come
upon you; and you will be my witnesses in Jerusalem, in all
Judea and Samaria, and to the ends of the earth (ACTS 1:8).

These passages speak to us of a great potential for a Christian: the
potential to rise above the usual to an abundant life, one empowered
by God and accompanied by signs and wonders. If the Word of
God is true, as we proclaim, specific results should be evident in our
lives as Jesus inferred when he said, "You will know them by their fruits"
(MATT. 7:20).

How do we account for the fact that such evidence of the power of
God is not as prominent in the body of Christ in our day as it was in
the early Christian church? What has contributed to this situation
characterized by fewer people becoming Christians? Lack of miraculous
healings, wise counsel, deliverances from bondage, and fewer dramat-
ically changed lives? What does the body of Christ need to be more
effective in ministering to the multitudes who are crying for assurance
of salvation, relief from pain, and help with a host of severe problems?

Because many feel that their needs are not being met through the
church, it is not surprising to see many turning in their desperation to
cults and non-Christian religions. They hope to find some kind of light
to lead them out of their hopelessness.

When the Christian church does not visibly demonstrate much fruitfulness, it becomes relatively easy for nonbelievers and skeptics to
conclude that there is no God.

The Christian church needs to do more than pass resolutions with
good intentions to serve and minister to people. Resolutions without
the resources to implement them bear no fruit. The Christian church
needs to demonstrate by its actions that it is proclaiming the life-
changing gospel: "the power of God for salvation" (ROM. 1:16).

In a lecture, Dr. James Burtness, a seminary professor, stated that
membership in mainline Christianity is declining because both clergy
and laity have "lost their nerve" (George Aus Memorial Lectures, March
13, 1985, Luther Northwestern Seminary, St. Paul). He stated that we

are also losing people on both sides of the center that mainline churches represent. We are losing people who want to live their lives with greater enthusiasm and commitment. We are losing people who are drifting out of the Christian church altogether because their needs are simply not being met.

Columnist Sydney J. Harris commented, "Societies need people they can look up to and emulate. A nation that does not reward and respect real accomplishments . . . is weakening its own moral fiber and preparing for its own collapse" ("Guess Who Kids Look Up to Most," *These Times*, January 1983).

In examining such statements we cannot help but wonder if the Christian church has not lost its attraction and power by casually slipping from its original moorings. Why such impotence? Why so few results?

We read with interest the promises that God made to his people in the past:

> The Lord your God will make you abundantly prosperous in all your undertakings, in the fruit of your body, in the fruit of your livestock, and in the fruit of your soil. For the Lord will again take delight in prospering you, just as he delighted in prospering your ancestors" (DEUT. 30:9).

While this is initially a promise of material prosperity, in reading on we are quick to discover that even this material prosperity is conditional. The following verse gives us the key to this material prosperity in one little word—"if":

> The Lord your God will make you abundantly prosperous in all the work of your hand. . . . If you obey the voice of the Lord your God, to keep his commandments and his statutes which are written in this book of the law, if you turn to the Lord your God with all your heart and with all your soul (DEUT. 30:9-10, RSV).

It is noteworthy that many promises in the Bible carry such a condition. The promises of God are going to be fulfilled when the conditions are met. Such a concept can easily be misunderstood and interpreted to mean that the key to prosperity—physical, emotional, and spiritual—

is to be totally obedient. We may think we have to earn what we receive from God.

We realize the impossibility of perfectly obeying all God's commandments. There is no way that by our own ability or wisdom we can either receive the blessings of God or use the blessings of God to minister to others. In the light of all the promises in God's Word, there appears to be yet more for us to experience than we have thus far experienced. How then can we who are contaminated with sin fulfill such requirements in order to receive the blessings? How can we experience the Spirit of God in our lives and share the blessings of God in a world that is in desperate need of help and is looking for some word of encouragement?

This makes us aware that we need to know how to appropriate what is available to us by the grace and mercy of God. We realize that it is impossible for us to create strength within ourselves by our own efforts to do anything. We find that we have questions. What are we capable of doing and what are we not capable of doing? What is our responsibility and where does God's grace fit in?

Therefore, it seems fitting that a book on gifts of the Holy Spirit begins with a close examination of the doctrine of grace. We will first look at what grace is, and also look at the concept of cheap grace, legalism, and libertinism.

When do the conditional "ifs" become a hindrance to the blessings that come to us through the grace and mercy of God? How are the "ifs" to be applied in a proper manner so they do not become legalistic abuses? When do they become examples of cheap grace? By reviewing these questions, we seek to learn how the grace of God may be free to function and restore people to wholeness.

The discussion above may lead us to raise the question, "Does grace imply that we need to do nothing but sit and wait?" In this book we will consider grace in relation to the gifts of the Holy Spirit in order to show that the grace of God is free to flow with all those gifts without causing division and disharmony in the body of Christ. God's grace and these gifts in all their variety will be better understood and practiced in the body of Christ. When they are, Christians will be able to be more effective in ministering to the multitudes of people who are desperately crying out in their sin, lostness, and pain, and who are longing for assurance of personal salvation.

The church can be more effective in its outreach if it utilizes all the gifts of the Spirit—including the charismatic gifts. "Charismatic gifts" refer to those gifts listed in Ephesians 4:11-12; Romans 12:6-8; 1 Corinthians 12:7-10, 27-31; and 1 Peter 4:10. Fear and uncertainty have often kept the church from utilizing all these gifts. One of the categories of gifts—the manifestational gifts (described in chap. 5)—includes insight, signs and wonders, and speaking in tongues. These gifts have often brought division and disharmony into a body of believers where they were introduced in a careless and overambitious manner. There is a sound, biblical way that all such gifts can be part of a congregation's life, one that does not bring disharmony or disunity. When practiced in the way in which Paul himself practiced them, they can enhance the effectiveness of the entire body of Christ. This book presents an orderly approach to the charismatic gifts. When charismatic gifts are fully understood, they can bring more effective ministry in and to the body of Christ.

It should be emphasized that both the content and method of this book presuppose the ongoing ministry of the Word and sacrament in the Christian community. In the theological and ecclesiastical tradition of the Evangelical Lutheran Church in America, as well as in other major Christian traditions, it is held that the Spirit and the gifts are imparted and enlivened by the proclamation of the Word and the administration of the sacraments. Therefore what follows cannot serve as a "quick fix" to any and all troubled situations. It is offered rather as a model for ministry in those very congregations where the Word and sacrament ministry, correctly done, has resulted in the manifestation of a variety of charismatic gifts and the need to understand them and how they relate to one another. Beyond that, if the ministry of Word and sacrament is not being exercised at the center of a congregation's life, it is necessary to restore or reform that ministry before anything that follows can possibly be of help.

QUESTIONS FOR DISCUSSION OR REFLECTION

1. Do you agree that the Christian church today could demonstrate more fruitfulness in ministry if it were better equipped and informed?

2. What have you heard about the *charismata*, the gifts of the Spirit, and what has been your experience with them?

3. Would you appreciate more teaching on the subject of charismatic gifts?

4. When you hear about charismatic gifts, do you usually think only of the mysterious ones like speaking in tongues, or do you realize that there are others such as mercy, wisdom, and administration?

PART ONE

Grace and the Gifts of the Holy Spirit

CHAPTER 1

Not By Your Own Doing

Basic Concerns

What can I do to be more effective in my Christian life?" "How can I be able to minister more effectively to others in my Christian walk?" "How might I be more effective in my Christian witness?" "Is there anything that I could be doing wrong that prevents a more direct or specific response to my prayers?" "What about the gifts of the Spirit? Is it possible for me to appropriate such gifts?" "Have I missed something along the way?" "What specifically are my gifts?"

These are some of the questions asked by individuals searching for a deeper walk with God who think that their lives and witness are not particularly Christlike or do not display much power. In evaluating their circumstances, they come to the conclusion that their situation must be due to some fault of theirs. As a result they may be led to some inaccurate conclusions regarding their abilities.

While it may be true that they have contributed to their own ineffectiveness, hopelessness, and despair in various ways, it may likewise be true that they have so focused on themselves and their shortcomings that they have forgotten a most important aspect of the Christian faith:

> "For by grace you have been saved through faith, and this is not your own doing; it is the gift of God—not the result of works, so that no one may boast" (EPH. 2:8-9).

These are significant words. We are saved by grace, by God's freely given mercy. However, grace does not abruptly stop with *justification*,

15

that is, being seen as righteous through faith in Christ. Grace embraces every area of the Christian life. Grace is also the key to *sanctification*—growth in holiness. Grace is the key to life and living. While the Spirit of God is the gift, grace is the means for all gifts to come to us. Grace is the key.

The doctrine of grace brought about the Reformation. The Reformation involved a rediscovery of grace in the New Testament by the reformers. For this reason our book begins by focusing on grace.

What Is Grace?

Where shall we begin in our discussion of grace? We can start by stating that grace is decisive for Christianity. Grace is the first chapter in Christianity. Without grace there is nothing but hopelessness, despair, and futility. Without grace there is nowhere to be and nowhere to go. For this reason a proper understanding of grace becomes essential to the whole of the Christian faith and life.

The word *grace* in Greek is *charis*, which is defined as that which affords joy, pleasure, delight, charm, goodwill, loving-kindness, and gratitude. The principal idea behind these words is that grace is a free gift from God intended to bring joy and blessing to the recipient. It is called "free" grace because it is not grounded in any worthiness of the individual. Any inference of merit as constituting a claim upon grace destroys its very meaning. Merit and grace are mutually exclusive. A proper understanding of grace is important because grace affects every aspect of the Christian life.

This gift not only applies to justification (being forgiven), but also to sanctification (growth in holiness after we experience forgiveness). It is meant to be a gift that will enable us to experience not only the blessing of eternal life in Christ Jesus, but also the work of the Spirit of Jesus that enables effective, fruitful service now.

In order to better understand grace, we could ask, "Who is God?" The Gospel of John specifically addresses that question and its answer as it relates to grace:

> In the beginning was the Word, and the Word was with God, and the Word was God. . . . And the Word became flesh and lived among us, and we have seen his glory, the glory as of a father's only son, full of grace and truth (JOHN 1:1, 14).

This tells us that Jesus is God in the flesh. Jesus is the person who is God. Jesus is grace personified. In and through the incarnation of God through Jesus Christ we see a manifestation of grace in the flesh. The life of Jesus is a tangible demonstration of grace to us. This is verified in the statement: "Grace and truth came through Jesus Christ" (JOHN 1:17).

In order to understand this we need to observe grace as revealed in all of God's Word, both Old and New Testaments. Let us observe how God's grace is revealed in the Old Testament.

Grace in the Old Testament

A search for the background of the New Testament word for grace (*charis*) is instructive. In the *Theological Dictionary of the New Testament* (Grand Rapids: Wm. B. Eerdmans, 1964-76, 9:389), Hans Conzelmann points out that the word *charis* is used in the Septuagint (a Greek version of the Hebrew Scriptures) as a translation of the Hebrew word *chen*. In *Grace and Faith in the Old Testament* (Minneapolis: Augsburg, 1980, p. 13) Ronald Hals asserts that although the Old Testament concept of *chen* does not attain the fullness of meaning that is associated with *charis* in the New Testament, the concept of a God who acts graciously is indeed apparent in the Old Testament. We see grace clearly manifested through God's merciful acts.

Hals says that we may not find the word *grace* in the Old Testament as often as we do in the New. He points out, however, that grace and salvation by grace through faith are also present in the Old Testament.

Throughout the Old Testament we find God gracious in his protection of Israel. Israel was attacked on every side by hostile enemies. Sometimes the odds were so great that the situation seemed hopeless, but in the midst of such circumstances are words of encouragement: "The Lord will fight for you" (EXOD. 14:14, 25).

There is a consistent emphasis on the gracious intervention of God. Perhaps the clearest example of God's grace in the Old Testament is the Exodus, the miraculous deliverance of the Israelites from the bondage of Egypt. The Song of Miriam and Moses celebrates that triumph, giving all credit to God:

> I will sing to the Lord, for he has triumphed gloriously; horse and rider he has thrown into the sea. The Lord is my strength

and my might, and he has become my salvation; this is my God, and I will praise him, my father's God, and I will exalt him (EXOD. 15:1-2).

The Lord once again graciously intervened when the Midianites sought to destroy the Israelites. God raised up a deliverer in Gideon, a man who was not particularly endowed with wisdom and other forms of charisma. We would likely classify him as average or even below average. His words confirm this estimation: "But sir, how can I deliver Israel? My clan is the weakest in Manasseh, and I am the least in my family" (JUDG. 6:15).

We readily see the weakness of Israel and Gideon and we also see the patience and grace of a loving God. God has a way of graciously gifting those who do not seem specifically endowed with unusual ability.

Gideon sought to bring deliverance to Israel by recruiting an army of thirty-two thousand men. But the Lord reduced that number to a mere three hundred. Furthermore, he removed their weapons and issued them trumpets, jars, and torches with which they were to defeat the enemy. God sometimes uses ordinary things to accomplish great purposes.

The reason for such apparent nonsensical action by God was to demonstrate divine grace as the source of the Israelites' victory and to prevent them from taking pride in their own ability and strength. We read, "Israel would only take the credit away from me, saying, 'My own hand has delivered me.' . . . For I have given it into your hand" (JUDG. 7:2, 9).

The writer of Judges repeatedly reminds us that the Lord is the one who graciously gave Israel the victory. God is a gracious God. In spite of the sins and shortcomings of the people, God loves, encourages, heals, protects, enables, saves, and delivers them. These are clear manifestations of God's grace.

The Israelites' deliverance and empowering comes as a gracious act of God's mercy. The children of Israel certainly did not earn or deserve God's love, encouragement, healing, protection, salvation, and deliverance.

We also see the grace of God demonstrated in those he chooses. We see this in his covenant relationship with the people. "I am the Lord your God" is the introduction to the Ten Commandments (EXOD. 20:2).

However, these words are much more than an introduction; they also are a declaration of God's grace. Sometimes we mistakenly consider this covenant relationship as one that was mutually decided between God and the Israelites, or we attribute something meritorious to the Israelites that provided God with the opportunity to pour out his grace upon them. While such may be wishful thinking, there is no substance in it. The Lord decided to choose, save, equip, and deliver Israel because he was and is a gracious God.

It may surprise us to find God's grace in the Ten Commandments and other expressions of his law, but it is there because a major purpose of the law is to provide guidance for fulfilled living. The law in reality is a demonstration of what is on the heart and mind of God. The law tells us what makes for happiness, for peace, for joy, for harmony, for unity, and for fulfilled living. The law is God's grace etched clearly on tablets of stone.

The law is God's graceful revelation of himself; his wisdom, his nature, his love, his attributes, and his desires. It reveals to us much of the nature and heart of God.

Later in this chapter we will see that the law has various functions. It reveals the grace of God as it discourages ungodliness, encourages order, convicts of sin, and also provides some guidance for fulfilled living.

Finally, we also see the grace of God in his judicial action. God has plans for his people because of his love for them. He longed for the best for them, yet all too frequently such gracious love was rebelliously rejected. The messages of the prophets ring clear with love but also with the judgment of God under such rebellious conditions:

> I reared children and brought them up, but they have rebelled
> against me. The ox knows its owner, and the donkey its
> master's crib; but Israel does not know, my people do not
> understand. . . . If you are willing and obedient, you shall eat
> the good of the land; but if you refuse and rebel, you shall be
> devoured by the sword; for the mouth of the Lord has spoken
> (ISA. 1:2-3, 19-20).

The heart of God longs to pour out his richest blessings on his people, but if they refuse and rebel God has threatened to take punitive measures on those who reject his grace. Evidence of this kind of judgment can be found in many places: "You are not my people and I am not your God" (HOS. 1:9); "I am going to give this city into the hand of the king of Babylon" (JER. 34:2).

But even as we read some of the strongest words of judgment, we are consistently also given a gracious message of hope. God never leaves his people in a state of condemnation without a word that brings some message of comfort. This is clearly a manifestation of God's grace in the midst of a message of judgment. Robert Hals asserts, "Judgment is only understood rightly when it is seen as a message of death, and the prophetic promises are rightly grasped only when they are heard as offering life out of death" (*Grace and Faith in the Old Testament*, Minneapolis: Augsburg, 1980, p. 76).

Grace in the New Testament

Now let us also look at grace as it is described in the New Testament. Naturally, the first person we look to for the use of the word *grace* (*charis*) is Jesus. The actual word *charis* is used four times in reference to Christ in Luke 1:30, 2:40, 52; and 4:22, where the emphasis is on goodwill and blessing. The only place in the four Gospels where grace is used in the sense of God's unmerited favor is in John 1:14, where Christ is declared to be full of grace (*charis*) and truth.

However, there are parables in the four Gospels that illustrate God's grace. Some of the best known are the parable of the lost sheep, the lost coin, the prodigal son, the Pharisee and the publican, and the great supper. Each of these parables demonstrates God's unconditional love, mercy, forgiveness, and patience, which are manifestations of his grace.

In addition, there is the beautiful account of the thief on the cross who in the final moment of his life cried out to Jesus: "Jesus, remember me when you come into your kingdom" (LUKE 23:42). The grace of Jesus is apparent when he replies that the thief would be with him in paradise (LUKE 23:43).

In the parables and in Jesus' words to the thief, the Gospels do not specifically use the word *grace*. However, the Gospels reveal to us the One who is grace personified. The Gospels allow the reader to observe Jesus, "see" grace in action, and experience the grace of God. In the life of Jesus we see grace in action, much as in the Old Testament we see grace in action through God's mercy.

The emphasis on grace is not proclaimed equally in all New Testament books. Jesus himself never used the word *grace* as such, but he was grace incarnate.

Paul introduced the word *grace* when the teaching surfaced that humanity in some way could earn the favor and blessing of God. It was said that the people would need first to fulfill the requirements of the law. Paul, seeing the dangerous tendency in such teaching, pointed out that salvation came not through any obedience to the words of the law but by grace through faith. We can see this emphasis most clearly in his writings to the Romans and Galatians.

The book of Acts provides us with a bridge from the Gospels to the Epistles; from the Lord of grace to the doctrine of grace. The early Christians recognized that the distinguishing feature of the gospel was grace and that it centered in Jesus. This is apparent when on the day of Pentecost the people came to Peter asking, "What shall we do?" Peter told them to repent and be baptized in the name of Jesus Christ so that their sins would be forgiven and that they would receive the gift of the Holy Spirit (ACTS 38:2).

He elaborated by saying, "For the promise is for you, and for your children." This reveals to us the grace of God not only through the forgiveness of sins but also through the gift of the Holy Spirit poured out on both adults and children. These gifts of forgiveness and the Holy Spirit are poured out freely not because of any merit on their part, but purely by the love and mercy of God that is a manifestation of his grace. However, Acts makes no specific attempt to specifically define grace. We get glimpses of grace through inference and example.

On the road to Damascus Paul confronted two great truths that he had dealt with previously, namely, that all is grace and grace is all. Paul experienced the reality of grace through his experience, first struck down with blindness and, later, having Ananias inform him that the Lord had sent him to minister healing to Paul. He became aware of his sinfulness and unworthiness and yielded to the Lord; he experienced not only forgiveness but also healing.

Paul became aware of his mistakes and only by God's grace was he privileged to experience God's great love and mercy. Through these experiences Paul came to understand the grace of God in his life. This entire confrontation is a clear demonstration of the grace of God in the life of a sinner who did nothing to deserve such grace.

Once Paul experienced the truth, he did not stop proclaiming it until his dying day. Paul frequently talks about the grace of God. Each one of his epistles either begins or ends (or both) with a salutation or benediction of grace. The most familiar ones are:

Grace to you and peace from God our Father and the Lord Jesus Christ (1 COR. 1:3; 2 COR. 1:2; GAL. 1:3).

The grace of the Lord Jesus be with you (1 COR. 16:23).

The grace of the Lord Jesus Christ, the love of God, and the communion of the Holy Spirit be with all of you (2 COR. 13:13).

The grace of the Lord Jesus Christ be with your spirit (PHIL. 4:23).

Grace be with all who have an undying love for our Lord Jesus Christ (EPH. 6:24).

Grace Is the Prerequisite

We have discovered that God's grace can be frequently found in both the Old and New Testaments. Justification and sanctification are gifts offered to all who accept them. These gifts are given to us purely by the unconditional love of God. Grace is a gift to us for both living and dying, for this world and the next.

Paul does not discuss the charismatic gifts (in Ephesians, Romans, and 1 Corinthians) until he clearly defines God's grace to his hearers and readers. This is especially apparent in the book of Romans where the first eight chapters deal almost exclusively with God's grace. Finally in chap. 12 we are introduced to the charismatic gifts.

It is impossible to separate grace from any aspect of the Christian life, whether it be justification, sanctification, or glorification. The grace of God makes all gifts possible. Therefore grace is intimately related to all gifts, including the charismatic gifts, which will be considered later in this book.

Grace has been gloriously manifested and revealed in and through Christ Jesus. Grace also empowers the life of the believer so that the grace of God manifests itself through the believing Christian in effective, influential witness. This is emphasized in passages such as this one:

For the grace of God has appeared, bringing salvation to all, training us to renounce impiety and worldly passions, and in the present age to live lives that are self-controlled, upright, and godly, while we wait for the blessed hope and the manifestation of the glory of our great God and Savior, Jesus Christ. He it is who gave himself for us that he might redeem us from all iniquity and purify for himself a people of his own who are zealous for good deeds (TITUS 2:11-14).

The Place of the Law

The Bible contains many commands. All were given by the grace of God for the well-being of his people. In the New Testament we are admonished, "Bear one another's burdens, and in this way you will fulfill the law of Christ" (GAL. 6:2).

Such a command has nothing to do with our salvation but has a great deal to do with fulfilled living. There is no question that our salvation is by grace alone. Yet those commands were given by the grace of God and if ignored or broken, there will be certain consequences. In this respect it is to our advantage to bear one another's burdens in order to fulfill the calling of God on our lives.

To ignore an exhortation like this is to invite the consequences: all of us may become burdened. By not helping the poor and needy to become self-sustaining, we allow even more people to be poor and needy in the future. By not sharing what I have in Christ I miss the blessing of sharing what I have in Christ.

For this reason we might be inclined to eat what we desire or choose to abstain from eating so as not to offend someone, as Paul informs us in 1 Corinthians 8. We have freedom, but we may choose not to exercise that freedom. That is in essence practicing real freedom. As Paul stated, "All things are lawful for me but not all things are beneficial" (1 COR. 6:12).

We realize that as we minister to each other in a loving manner by the grace of God, we also experience blessing, harmony, and unity. Therefore, I willingly choose to follow "the law of Christ" so that I might experience the blessing that he longs to pour out to me. As we demonstrate our trust in God through faith and obedience, we experience the reality of the law of Christ. Thus the grace of God expresses itself in love and compassion through the faith of the believer. As Frederick Bruner says in his book A Theology of the Holy Spirit,

Faith, which is the work of the Spirit, evidences itself, in
Paul's unforgettable expression it "energizes" itself in love (*pistis
di agapes energoumene,* Galatians 5:6b.) Christian love requires
the energy of the Spirit. This energy is received by faith
(Grand Rapids: Wm. B. Eerdmans, 1982, p. 274).

This indicates that in our own strength we are not able to come up
with the ability to be obedient and faithful. Yet, we are encouraged
that God, who sets the standards, graciously provides the strength that
is necessary to enable us to be obedient in the various circumstances
that come our way. God does not make unreasonable demands that
only leave people frustrated and hopeless. He comes to our rescue by
sending his Holy Spirit who empowers us to be what he calls us to be.
This also is a clear expression of God's grace.

Beginning at our baptism the Spirit of God is poured into us as
helpless children, empowering us to be faithful to the laws of God. We
are brought to a gracious God who does a mysterious work in us to
make us his own. It is already with such humble beginnings and in
such a helpless condition that the Spirit of God begins his gracious
work—a work that stretches beyond our fondest expectations. It is a
mystery that does not lend itself to rational thought. In his book *Spiritus
Creator,* Regin Prenter states,

The work of the Spirit is a miracle. We have seen how the
experiment of inner conflict permits no other understanding of
the Spirit's work. In inner conflict man is completely in the
power of death. Nothing of his own righteousness is effective.
The groaning of the Spirit toward God is a real raising from
death, a new creation. When the gospel says that no one can
enter the Kingdom of God without the new birth of water and
the Spirit it simply means that the old man must be destroyed
totally. The old man must become as the earth which was
waste and void before the first creation so that God the Holy
Spirit can create the new man out of nothing (Philadelphia:
Fortress Press, 1953, p. 185).

The purpose for this "work of the Spirit" is that I might be "set apart"
to be assured of my salvation and glorify the Father through faithful
service. His grace enables and empowers me for this blessed task of

witnessing to the love of God in Christ. As stated, there is no way that we can save ourselves or minister in our own strength to the multitudes that do not yet know Christ.

God's Word extends beyond the boundaries of the past. It is relevant to the present in the same way that it was in the past, for Jesus is "the same yesterday and today and forever" (HEB. 13:8).

His grace is still being poured out. Because he is still the same, we believe it is Jesus who is still able and willing to continue his good work. We do not need more human reason or human opinions. We do not need more willpower, more knowledge, more condemnation, or anything else that the world may have to offer. What we need most is more of Jesus, for having more of him will help us realize more of his grace. We are informed, "the Word became flesh and lived among us . . . full of grace and truth" (JOHN 1:14).

Jesus is full and complete, lacking in nothing. He is self-sufficient, full of grace and truth. This grace is still poured out and is sufficient for every need of those who submit to the claims of Jesus Christ. "And my God will fully satisfy every need of yours according to his riches in glory in Christ Jesus" (PHIL. 4:19).

Our desire, therefore, ought to be for more and more of Christ's Spirit. For as we come to a more intimate relationship with him we also experience more and more of his grace to witness, minister, and serve. But in order to keep this longing from becoming only an exercise in legalism on the one hand and cheap grace on the other, it is important for us to examine those extremes so as to retain proper direction in our Christian faith and life.

Legalism and Cheap Grace

Occasionally the question arises, "How do all these words about grace apply to me?" "Am I obliged to do anything?" "Does God's grace force me to do anything?" The answer of course is that I am not obliged to do anything and God's grace does not force me to do anything to earn salvation. But the fact that we are Christians does not free us from the law of God. It is true that we are delivered from its sentence by virtue of the death of Christ, but the law of God still plays an important role in our lives.

The Book of Concord, a Lutheran document, describes three uses of the law. The first is the civil use of the law. This use is intended to discourage ungodliness and to provide order in a world of sinful individuals. The second is the theological use, which is intended to make people aware of their sinfulness, ungodliness, and disobedience and lead them to repent. The third use is that the law is to be a guide for Christian living.

When people become Christians, a new power begins to operate in their lives. Theirs is a resurrection life. Empowered by the risen Christ, they feel his power flow through them. They have been baptized into Christ Jesus (ROM. 6:3-4), the Son of God, who lived a perfect life. This Jesus proceeds to give to all the "Spirit of life" (ROM. 8:2). What does this mean for a Christian's daily life? Paul explains,

> For God has done what the law, weakened by the flesh, could not do: by sending his own Son in the likeness of sinful flesh, and to deal with sin, he condemned sin in the flesh, so that the just requirement of the law might be fulfilled in us, who walk not according to the flesh but according to the Spirit (ROM. 8:3-4).

This indicates that we Christians are not finished with the law of God. We no longer are under its sentence, its condemnation, because God's Son took care of that. Yet we cannot avoid the law's standards. This indicates that holiness or sanctification is not an option, but rather the next step. We are urged, "May the God of peace himself sanctify you entirely" (1 THESS. 5:23). We are urged to allow the Spirit of God to fill our lives so that our lives are holy, loving, and self-giving.

However, such an admonition and exhortation to live holy lives can cause us to misunderstand, indeed, abuse grace. One such abuse is legalism. Another is cheap grace. Both extremes devalue the importance of Jesus' life, death, and resurrection for us. A clear understanding of grace is crucial to help avoid both legalism and cheap grace.

Cheap grace, or thinking that God's gift of salvation through Christ didn't cost him anything, is often considered to be the opposite of legalism. Related to cheap grace is libertinism, which has been defined as dissolute or licentious conduct. Some think that if salvation is so free (cheap), then what they do doesn't matter. It is taking grace to the extreme left. They take advantage of grace, believing every kind of practice is acceptable because they are saved by grace. They conclude that there are no restrictions on how they live their lives; sanctification or holiness are not even considered. Therefore, they believe they can indulge in all kinds of questionable, ungodly living without being personably accountable in the Christian walk.

Legalism has been defined in several ways: living according to laws to demonstrate worthiness, trying to earn God's favor through one's own efforts, seeking salvation through works rather than grace, emphasizing external form over the importance of the inner spirit, insisting on strict application of rules without proper regard to specific circumstances, and demanding one's own type of righteousness from another. It is making the form the objective. Legalism loses the goal of Christianity.

Legalism is often associated with the law. It takes grace to the extreme right. It has so many restrictions that there is no freedom. It is as if Christ's death and resurrection were meaningless. Life is one continual encumbrance of laws. Hardly anything can be done without some type of confrontation with specific laws about one's behavior.

Many people believe that any reference to law, even in connection with grace or charismatic gifts, is legalism, that is, having to earn God's favor. This is not true.

Laws of one sort or another have been in existence from the beginning of time. They were not invented as legalistic maneuvers that we can ignore without consequences. For example, if we should choose to deny that the law of gravity exists, proceed to ignore it, and jump from a building, that choice would not render the law of gravity void or without effect. Nor does it make the law of gravity legalistic. It simply indicates that this law exists and those who choose to go against it will suffer the consequences.

The laws of God are for this life only. When we arrive at our eternal home there will no longer be any need for the law, for it will have fulfilled its purpose. Theologian Gerhard Forde describes the law's function in this way:

> The law and its office or function is therefore strictly limited to this age. It is an accuser. That is its chief function, its office. As accuser it stands inviolate, unrelenting, without any "veil," until that to which it points arrives. As long as sin and death remain, the law remains. Unfaith, sin, death and the law are inseparable partners, until the ultimate triumph of the eschatological kingdom, the law will sound (*Forensic*

Justification by Faith, Minneapolis: Augsburg, 1985, pp. 300–301).

Laws can help us to see something of the mind and will of God. They can also demonstrate God's love and grace. However, the law remains an objective entity and it does not change because of our attitudes toward it. Christians continue to face the law and its demands. But there is a distinct difference in the attitude of Christians as they consider the law. What is our motive as Christians to be obedient?

> Now therefore, if you obey my voice and keep my covenant, you shall be a treasured possession out of all the peoples. Indeed, the whole earth is mine, but you shall be to me a priestly kingdom and a holy nation (EXOD. 19:5-6).

This indicates that God's grace was demonstrated in his action in the Old Testament. He delivered, freed, loved, healed, and rescued his people after which he issued his laws to them in the hope that this manifestation of his love would motivate them to respond in faithful obedience. From the beginning God was faithful in revealing his grace.

God's Word informs us that God has blessed us in Christ with every spiritual blessing (EPH. 1:3). In light of God's grace to us in Christ Jesus, a natural response is that we become motivated to lead lives that are godly, moral, and righteous, thereby glorifying God even through our lives: "Lead a life worthy of the calling to which you have been called" (EPH. 4:1). "For the love of Christ urges us on, because we are convinced that one died for all; therefore all have died (2 COR. 5:14).

Charles Caldwell Ryrie summarizes this well when he states,

> Correct conduct is motivated today by blessings already received. This is an unalterable order. Thus the motive cannot be legalism. One could say that he will live for the Lord in order to be blessed, but since we have already been blessed with all spiritual blessings, no amount of good works can add to that fact. Man's perversion of the true motive then may be closely related to legalism, but since there is only one true motive, then technically the motive cannot be legalism (*The Grace of God*, Chicago: Moody Press, 1963, p. 75).

The basic motive for righteousness and holiness is the love of God in Christ Jesus. In gratefulness we seek to respond accordingly. But this desire to respond in itself can also become a subtle means of becoming enslaved under the law. This enslavement is brought about when we hear a message, which, indirectly or directly, gives the impression that we are paying for salvation on the installment plan. An example would be if we believe that we are saved by grace but that we must pay for it later through our gratitude. To some this may appear sound, but it is obviously erroneous. Therefore, we need to look both forward and backward in order to understand grace completely. We need to look backward at what Christ has done, which ought to motivate us to gratitude. But we must also look forward, first to know that "nothing good dwells within me, that is, in my flesh" (ROM. 7:18).

We also need to look forward to the high call that Christ sets before us. Then we realize that gratitude alone will not provide the power. We must trust in the mighty working of the Holy Spirit to enable us in all things. This is apparent from these words:

> Therefore I want you to understand that no one speaking by the Spirit of God ever says "Let Jesus be cursed!" and no one can say "Jesus is Lord" except by the Holy Spirit (1 COR. 12:3).

When we fail to live up to our high calling as Christians, it is not for a lack of gratitude, but for lack of trusting the grace and power of the Holy Spirit who enables us in our gratitude, worship, service, and outreach. Knowing that sanctification is also a work of grace is important lest we fall into a legalistic practice with best intentions. Legalism may produce outward results similar to sanctification, but such results are poor imitations.

Legalism invariably leaves a person with a lack of fulfillment or lasting results. Legalists know what is commanded and will likely do it because they know it needs to be done. Therefore, they will do it but without a proper motive or attitude. The existence of laws in itself does not produce legalism, but an attitude that seeks to bring merit to oneself is legalistic.

A good example of such a legalistic attitude is found in the account of the publican and Pharisee. Both were aware of the law. Both went up to the temple to pray. But each man came with a different attitude.

The Pharisee came with an attitude that sought to bring honor and glory to himself which is apparent from his self-righteous prayer:

> God, I thank you that I am not like other people; thieves, rogues, adulterers, or even like this tax collector. I fast twice a week, I give a tenth of all my income (LUKE 18:11-12).

His legalistic life-style was not motivated by gratefulness for the blessings of God in his life, but rather by his desire to build up his pride and bring attention to his own accomplishments.

On the other hand, the publican was aware of his own shortcomings. He pleaded for mercy, and Jesus tells us that this man received what he requested: "All who humble themselves will be exalted" (LUKE 18:14).

The motivation behind legalism is to bring glory to ourselves, and giving honor to something or someone other than God is idolatry. When the self is elevated to such a position of honor and praise, we have idolatry.

Idolatry is not tolerated by God because it replaces God with someone or something other than God. It presents a conflict because grace is not allowed to function as God intended. An idolatrous attitude readily presents problems in expressions of charismatic gifts because the opportunity for self-glorification surfaces. Charismatic gifts used for purposes of self-glorification invariably lead to divisiveness.

At the other extreme from legalism is libertinism. We have established that law is everywhere. Yet libertinism is the attempt to live without any restraints of the law, and those following it believe that a Christian is totally free from the law.

This raises another question: "How can we live in Christian freedom without going to the extremes in our freedom?" Paul and John emphasized not only the grace that is ours in Christ Jesus, but also the freedom with responsibility that is ours in Christ when they said,

> "For freedom Christ has set us free. Stand firm, therefore, and do not submit again to a yoke of slavery" (GAL. 5:1).

> "And you will know the truth, and the truth will make you free. . . . So if the son makes you free, you will be free indeed" (JOHN 8:32, 36).

"But now that you have been freed from sin and enslaved to God, the advantage you get is sanctification. The end is eternal life" (ROM. 6:22).

The most important aspect of Christian liberty is our justification by grace through faith in Christ Jesus. In this declaration of God's grace God demonstrates his love for us by claiming us as his children.

Christian liberty does not mean that we are allowed to do anything we please. Rather, it is an opportunity to demonstrate Christlikeness by and through faithfulness in our lives. Paul makes this clear when he states,

> What then are we to say? Should we continue in sin in order that grace may abound? By no means! How can we who died to sin go on living in it? . . . We have been buried with him by baptism into death, so that, just as Christ was raised from the dead by the glory of the Father, so we too might walk in newness of life (ROM. 6:1-2, 4).

> Having been set free from sin, [we] have become slaves of righteousness (ROM. 6:18).

It is characteristic of our day to interpret freedom to be a freedom that allows us to walk in sin and to think that Christian freedom puts no restrictions on how we live or what we do. The result is that often the world sees no difference between those who are Christians and those who are not. For it sees Christians practice the same kind of questionable behavior as those who do not profess to be Christians. This situation presents a confusing message to the entire world. Grace brings with it responsibility motivated out of love for God. Ryrie addresses this when he says,

> Justification liberty is not freedom to be saved in any way that man may please: sanctification liberty is not license to live as we choose; nor is glorification liberty other than freedom from the bondage of the presence of sin so that we may give wholehearted praise and service to God through eternity. . . . For unrestricted liberty is license, and wrongly restricted liberty

is legalism. Rightly restricted liberty is limited by love. (*The Grace of God*, Chicago: Moody Press, 1963, p. 81).

Paul sees through the facades that so often manifest themselves in rationalizations. Ultimately, these are nothing more than the desire to live as a pagan. A person who has been baptized into Jesus Christ and endowed and anointed with the Spirit of Christ is called to exhibit some Christlike qualities. He or she is not to walk in sin, but is expected to exhibit the fruit of righteousness and holiness. The Spirit of Christ puts into a Christian a different calling as Paul states,

> For you were called to freedom, brothers and sisters; only do not use your freedom as an opportunity for self-indulgence, but through love become slaves to one another. For the whole law is summed up in a single commandment, "You shall love your neighbor as yourself" (GAL. 5:13-14).

Much of what is practiced under the label of Christian freedom is not Christian love, but simply the selfish desire to live contrary to the Word of God. Living in ungodliness is not liberty but a continuation of bondage demonstrated by such living. Drunkards, gluttons, embezzlers, gossipers, and others may think that they have the Christian liberty to continue to their hearts' content but they ultimately end up in bondage to what they celebrated as liberation. This is demonstrated clearly in Romans 6-8.

Christians who are truly liberated in love and gratitude for what Christ has done by his grace are willing to give up whatever is harmful or unloving. This action is a living demonstration of the grace of God, manifested in the lives of those who are truly free.

Christian freedom is not an unrestricted liberty. It is rather a yielding to the Spirit of God. It allows Christ to direct our lives. Then the grace of God will be lived out in the manner in which God intended.

The gospel becomes the guide for Christian living. It is as Forde states:

> Because the gospel reigns absolutely in the conscience, the Christian is free so that the true battle can be joined in the flesh. The new being is not therefore a kind of mystical *theologoumenon* without substance but is to be incarnated in

concrete earthly fashion in the vocation of the Christian in this world. In this battle the commandments of God can be seen ultimately not as an enemy nor as a mere emasculated guide but as a real friend (*Forensic Justification by Faith*, Minneapolis: Augsburg, 1985, p. 303).

Christian freedom is freedom to be Christlike, freedom to love. Christlike love is demonstrating kindness to and concern for others. Christlike love is ministering to those who are in need of ministry. The world's idea of "love" is not love at all if it is carried out contrary to the will and Word of God.

Furthermore, the definition of love is not decided on the basis of what a few people might determine it to be. Such love would have no consistency because it would change with every breeze that blows. Its path would be littered with the fragments of broken relationships and rejected friends. True love that has its roots in the grace of God in Christ Jesus reaches to the very heart of God. Such love gives itself as a servant of righteousness. This is clearly demonstrated to us in the life of Christ as we read, "Who . . . did not count equality with God a thing to be grasped, but emptied himself, taking the form of a servant" (PHIL. 2:6-7, RSV).

Christian freedom then is the freedom to be Christlike. It is a freedom to be willing to surrender rights, privileges, positions, and places as needed in order to serve God and others rather than self.

Such liberty guided by Christlike love is not a demonstration of license or legalism, but of Christian liberty that is motivated to glorify God. Such Christian freedom moves boldly forward by faith in God through Christ to witness, to minister, to love, to deliver, and to heal.

This discussion brings us next to the responsibility of a person who has experienced the grace of God in Christ.

Allowing God's Grace to Flow Through Us

Manifestations of signs, wonders, and miracles seem to be taking place among the less educated and less prosperous in Third World countries. A pastor from India and some of his friends visited and shared their experiences in our church. They related many instances of a miraculous nature that had taken place among them in India. Sight was restored to the blind. The lame began to walk. Malignant tumors disappeared. All these manifestations took place after they had laid hands on sick people, prayed, and anointed them with oil as instructed according to James 5:13-18. Multitudes of people have turned to the Christian faith because they saw a power that they had not experienced before. The pastor was not arrogant or presumptuous, but in a humble, quiet manner talked about these things as if they were common manifestations among them.

While visiting mission fields in Third World countries, I was surprised to find that bishops regularly encourage their pastors and Bible workers to practice the laying on of hands and anointing with oil as they minister to the sick. They had no qualms about using such practices but considered them to be practices encouraged in the Word of God.

I conversed with a young black African Christian who was studying theology in one of our Lutheran seminaries. He stated that some African Christians were planning to send missionaries to the United States. Recently I once again heard the same comment from a bishop from one of the African churches while attending the International Charismatic Consultation on World Evangelism in Brighton, England. They believed there is a great need to evangelize the United States populace, which is not giving much evidence that it is Christian.

He went on to state that Christians in the United States have a Christianity that is more centered in the mind than in the heart and, as a result, it is not readily applied to the basic problems of life. The sermons and teachings from American pulpits seem more mental exercises than life experiences. The result is that little of the miraculous takes place to help people with their problems and illnesses and to attract the attention of the non-Christian world to witness to the power that could be manifested. The African Christian stated that he thought that Christianity needed to demonstrate more of the power of God through Christian life experiences. Some of this may be hard for us to receive, because we in First World nations have always felt somewhat superior. Yet we need to weigh this man's words carefully to discern whether they might contain more than a bit of truth.

Why are such manifestations of God's grace often more apparent among the less sophisticated and prosperous? Does their very simplicity become an asset to them when they step out in faith? What is the ingredient in their faith that enables them to experience what so often escapes us? Has our intellectualism become an obstacle that keeps us from moving into any area that does not lend itself to our kind of rational thinking? Have we fashioned for ourselves a golden calf while the unsophisticated are on Mt. Sinai hearing the Word of the Lord, acting on it, and experiencing blessings?

All too often these marvelous manifestations of God's grace become clouded rather than clarified by rational consideration. After some deliberation, they are often rejected as some kind of aberration of the mind. The result is that we who are sophisticated and rational may be impoverished while the humble who exercise simple, undaunted faith may experience many blessings and become wiser. The key to this dilemma for us may well be found in these words of Paul:

> When I came to you, brothers and sisters, I did not come proclaiming the mystery of God to you in lofty words or wisdom. For I decided to know nothing among you except Jesus Christ, and him crucified. And I came to you in weakness and in fear and in much trembling. My speech and my proclamation were not with plausible words of wisdom, but with a demonstration of the Spirit and of power, so that your faith might rest not on human wisdom but on the power of God (1 COR. 2:1-5).

Those who have experienced the grace of God ought also to rely on the Spirit and the power of God. The grace of God was not meant to be armored and locked away in rational thinking to protect itself from embarrassment. While rational thinking is also a gift, it is not the only gift. Rational thinking and openness to signs and wonders need to complement each other to be effective. The temptation is always to one extreme or the other and extremes usually bring major problems.

The bottom line comes back to the response of those who have experienced God's grace in Christ. When we have experienced the grace of God in our lives, how do we allow such grace to flow through us to others to demonstrate that God is still relevant and alive? Paul Tillich writes in one of his messages on healing,

> The gospels, certainly, are not responsible for this disappearance of power in the picture of Jesus. They abound in stories of healing; but we are responsible, ministers, laymen, theologians, who forgot that "Savior" means "healer," he who makes whole and sane what is broken and insane, in body and

mind. The woman who encountered Him was made whole, the demoniac who met Him was liberated from his mental cleavage. Those who are disrupted, split, disintegrated, are healed by him. And because this is so, because this power has appeared on earth, the kingdom of God has come upon us; this is the answer Jesus gives to the Pharisees when they discuss his power of healing the mentally possessed; this is the answer He gives to the Baptist to overcome his doubts; This is the order He gives to His disciples when He sends them to the towns of Israel. "And as you go, preach, saying, the kingdom of God is at hand. Heal the sick, raise the dead, cleanse the lepers, cast out demons." That is what they shall do and for this He gives them authority and power; for in Him the kingdom of God has appeared, and its nature is salvation, healing of that which is ill, making whole what is broken (*The New Being*, New York: Charles Scribner's Sons, 1955, pp. 43-44).

In order for us to experience more of the signs, wonders, and miracles of God, we need to step out and demonstrate a living, vibrant, practicing faith. We need to become fools for Christ (1 COR. 1:17-21).

What does it mean to become a fool for Christ? It means to step out in faith, even when there is the possibility that there might be no support as we attempt to witness to the love of God in Christ. We may stand alone while many sit and ridicule. Some of the greatest manifestations of God's grace come when we step out in faith and follow through on some action that seems unreasonable, unscientific, and out of the ordinary. It might not have been easy for Peter to step out onto the water (MATT. 14:22-33) knowing that if he faltered and went swimming, the other apostles could be quick to ridicule. There might also have been ridicule if he had kept walking on the water. Who was he to emulate Jesus?

We read with interest how the early Christians did not hesitate to proclaim what was theirs by the grace of God in Christ Jesus. They were bold and yet humble enough to become fools for the sake of Jesus Christ and the gospel. The key to such power is to be humble enough to be a fool for Christ as Paul states in the following passages:

Do not deceive yourselves. If you think that you are wise in this age, you should become fools so that you may become wise (1 COR. 3:18).

What have you that you did not receive? If then you received
it, why do you boast as if it were not a gift? Already you are
filled! Already you have become rich! Without us you have
become kings! And would that you did reign, so that we might
share the rule with you! For I think that God has exhibited us
apostles as last of all, like men sentenced to death; because we
have become a spectacle to the world, to angels and to men.
We are fools for Christ's sake (1 COR. 4:7-10, RSV).

The point is this: It is one thing to experience the grace of God in
Christ, but it is another to act upon that grace. Of what value is grace
with all its manifestations if it never becomes apparent in the lives of
those who have experienced it? How can we expect the extraordinary
if we are content with the ordinary? We are saved by grace, but "saved"
is a much broader and wider term than most of us have thought it to
be. What are the parameters of "saved" for us?

The Greek word for "saved," *sozo,* is a broad term which means "to
save, to keep from harm, to preserve, to rescue, to free from disease,
to deliver from demonic possession, to thrive, to prosper, to get well,"
and more. This list indicates that much is available to us through the
gracious mercy of God. This grace that we so enjoy and frequently take
for granted extends into all areas of our life both for now and for all
eternity. People from the moment of the Fall have had a need to be
saved, healed, and delivered from bondage. It was and is for this reason
that people look for the Savior, the healer. Tillich expresses this when
he says,

As in ours, so in the period of Jesus much talk was going on of
sickness, and healing. Jews and Greeks wrote about it. People
felt that they lived in a sick period; they called it "this world-
period" and they described it in a way which is very similar to
the way in which we describe it today. They saw not only the
bodily infirmity of all of us, the innumerable bodily diseases in
the masses of the people, they also saw the destructive powers
possessing the minds of many. . . . Out of this knowledge of a
sick period the question of a new period, a reality of health
and wholeness was asked. Salvation and a Savior were
expected. But salvation is healing. And the Savior is the

healer (*The New Being*, New York: Charles Scribner's Sons, 1955, pp. 36-37).

We find the same interest in our day in divine manifestations as is evidenced by the large number of individuals who are enrolled and wait to enroll in courses like one at Fuller Theological Seminary entitled "Signs, Wonders, and Church Growth." C. Peter Wagner, in "Signs and Wonders Today," reports that even though there has been some controversy regarding the course, there continues to be great interest in it. The catalog describes the course as focusing

> on understanding the effects of supernatural signs and wonders on the growth of the church. It is approached from biblical, theological, historical and contemporary perspectives. Special attention is given to the ministry of healing. Field experience is an important dimension of the course (*Signs and Wonders Today*, Wheaton, Ill.: Christian Life Missions, 1982).

So many students are interested in taking the course that it is always full, with a waiting list besides. Students are eager to learn about ministry in its broadest sense. The popularity of this course indicates a great interest in discerning how to appropriate everything available to us by the grace of God.

Our calling as children of God includes allowing the Spirit of God to flow freely from our lives to minister God's grace to others who have a need. This is specifically taught by Jesus in such parables as the Good Samaritan, at the conclusion of which he states, "Go and do likewise" (LUKE 10:30-37).

We cannot allow the Spirit of God to fill our entire being with grace and blessing and yet overlook the needs of the multitudes. For this reason Christians everywhere need to be encouraged and sent into this ministry of proclaiming the love of God in Christ. As people are healed, liberated, and set free from their hurts, they are attracted to the Christian faith and find their lives fulfilled. This sets in motion the entire cycle of evangelistic outreach because they in turn reach out to others.

The basic purpose of God's grace is to save, sanctify, and liberate his people, to set them free to love him and be his ambassadors. Christianity is a demonstration of being born and of bearing. Jesus was born and then proceeded to bear the burden of all our sins and shortcomings.

We are born and born again so that we might be the bearers of the good news that is ours in Christ Jesus. Much of the gospel is summarized in that one word—*born*—a word that communicates new life.

When a Christian professes to be born again as a child of God, experiences God's grace, and is not moved to bear the burdens of others who are brothers and sisters in Christ, we have some doubt as to the integrity of that Christian's confession. The apostle put it bluntly when he said that faith, if it has no works, is dead (JAMES 2:17). It is as Dietrich Bonhoeffer states,

> Surely he has born our griefs, and carried our sorrows . . . the chastisement of our peace was upon him. (ISA. 53:4-5)
> Therefore, the Bible can also characterize the whole life of the Christian as bearing the Cross. It is the fellowship of the Cross to experience the burden of the other. If one does not experience it, the fellowship he belongs to is not Christian. If any member refuses to bear that burden, he denies the law of Christ (*Life Together*, New York: Harper and Brothers, 1954, pp. 100-101).

Bonhoeffer's words emphasize that God's grace extends beyond the boundaries of the past. It is relevant to the present in the same way that it was in the past, for Jesus is "the same yesterday, today, and forever" (HEB. 13:8). It therefore becomes a responsibility of those who experience God's grace to put into practice the blessings and gifts they have received and experienced through the work of the Spirit of God in their lives.

Putting gifts into practice involves taking risks, becoming fools for Christ, and also making mistakes. Nevertheless, we march forward trusting that the grace that has brought us to this point in our lives is sufficient also to radiate out through us to bless the lives of many.

In spite of all the possibilities of sin, failure, and even the idolatry of self-exaltation, we need to march forward in faith. Our faith is demonstrated as the power of God manifests itself in whatever way that God chooses in order to bring healing, deliverance, counsel, guidance, and saving grace to those who cross our path.

While God's grace provides us with the assurance of salvation for all eternity, it is also meant to provide us with blessings for the present circumstances in life. Therefore, we need to step out in faith with the grace that is available to us and allow the grace of God in Christ Jesus to flow through us to touch damaged lives. This is best done by bringing to the lost the assurance of salvation; to the poor, food, clothing and shelter; and to the hurting, healing, deliverance, counsel, guidance, and comfort.

As we step out in faith, the scriptural promise "But each of us was given grace according to the measure of Christ's gift" (EPH. 4:7) becomes a reality for us. For grace is the means through which the gifts come to us.

We then become ready to allow God's grace to continue to take us even deeper into the reality of his presence and grace. In his book *When the Well Runs Dry*, Thomas Green describes various stages of prayer that Teresa of Avila used to allow the grace of God to flow more readily so that she could experience more of the blessings of God. He quotes her autobiography in relating the second stage of prayer, the Prayer of Quiet. She says,

> Let us now speak of the second way of drawing [water] which is ordained by the Lord of the garden. By using a device of windlass and buckets the gardener draws more water with less labor and is able to take some rest instead of being continuously at work. It is this method, applied to the prayer called the Prayer of Quiet, that I now wish to describe.

> This state, in which the soul begins to recollect itself, borders on the supernatural, to which [the soul] could in no way attain by its own exertions. True, it sometimes seems to have been wearied by its work at the windlass—its laboring with the understanding and its filling of the buckets; but in this state the water is higher and thus much less labor is required than for the drawing of it from the well. I mean that the water is nearer to [the soul], for grace reveals itself to the soul more clearly (quoted in *When the Well Runs Dry*, Notre Dame, Ind.: Ave Maria Press, 1985, pp. 36, 4511).

When we do this we avail ourselves to whatever gifts the Lord may pour out to us by his grace. The Holy Scriptures describe one such group of gifts that enable service and ministry under the name *charismata*. The relation of these to the principles of grace will be our next consideration.

QUESTIONS FOR DISCUSSION OR REFLECTION

1. What was your experience as you studied the Old Testament as you were growing up? Were you aware of the many examples of God's grace in the Old Testament?

2. What similarities do you see between grace in the Old Testament and grace in the New Testament? What differences?

3. What is the purpose of the law for Christians? Is a discussion of the three uses of the law (pages 25-26) helpful to Christian living? Why?

4. When have you experienced or observed libertinism? Legalism? How can a Christian remain well-balanced between the two extremes?

5. What have you heard about or experienced in regard to miracles or healings? Do you think they are more likely to be manifested among the less educated and less prosperous? Why or why not?

CHAPTER 2

The Immeasurable Riches of God's Grace

In Search of Truth

Grace is the means through which we are enabled to experience the blessings of God. Such blessings include the charismata—those gifts of the Spirit described in Ephesians 4:11-12; Romans 12:6-8; 1 Corinthians 12:7-10, 27-31; and 1 Peter 4:10—but our basic intent is to apply the principles of God's grace also to the charismata in order to make them practical and relevant for our lives.

Life often presents us with difficult situations and circumstances. At times it seems saturated with paradoxes. What appears to be appropriate at one time is not appropriate at another. What works on one occasion may not function well at all in another.

Circumstances and environment also play a role in determining what may be appropriate and what is not. This may cause frustration and disillusionment. It may also lead to discouragement and confusion and cause us to wonder, are we on the right track or are we wandering on a path to disaster? Are we progressing in our walk to spiritual maturity or are we regressing into spiritual infancy?

People may long for more of Christ, but more of Christ may also make life more difficult. Christlikeness often becomes offensive to the world. People may desire to exercise their Christian liberty but that very liberty may bring consequences that cause suffering. People long to be with people, but the more they are with them, the more they experience conflict with them. They all too quickly realize they are looking for the perfect among the imperfect. Similarly, if they should find the perfect and become associated with it, it would immediately become imperfect. It is so easy for people to pinpoint the shortcomings of others, yet be oblivious to their own. This is part of the difficulty that confronts us: sinners living with sinners. It does not take long to discover shortcomings in close relationships such as those we often experience in the body of Christ, the church.

It is such experiences in life that bring about an even greater longing for more of all that is available to us by the grace of God in terms of love, patience, power, peace, joy, ability, and fulfillment. It is this fulfillment that enables this entire process of peaceful, harmonious, meaningful life and living for time and for eternity.

Along with such longing for fulfilled living come also experiences of confusion and error. Those in search of such truth, unfortunately, will also find themselves from time to time in the uncomfortable position of error.

The search for truth produces various results and experiences. Not all mysterious experiences prove to be heretical or erroneous. Some of these that are legitimate have come to be known as charismatic experiences. For this reason careful study is needed—as well as research, prayer, and evaluation—to determine what is legitimate and what is questionable.

In the past charismatic experiences were often ignored and attributed to sects, cults, and fringe groups. However, in our generation, people who have had various charismatic experiences have moved into mainline denominations in such sizeable numbers that they have come to be considered one of the influential religious movements in this century.

The *Minneapolis Star and Tribune* (April 23, 1987) reported that estimates of the number of charismatics run as high as 10 million people. More recent information from the church historian David Barrett in *The World Christian Encyclopedia* (New York: Oxford University Press, 1986, p. 839) says that the estimates run as high as 30 million.

If we should ignore such a movement, we will only invite negative consequences for everyone, both in our country and in our church. Perhaps it might be wise to follow the advice of the old sage Gamaliel, as we read, "If this plan or this undertaking is of human origin, it will fail; but if it is of God, you will not be able to overthrow them" (ACTS 5:38-39).

The mainline Protestant and Catholic charismatic movement began around 1960. In the span of less than two decades the movement spread to every continent of the globe and into every major Christian denom-ination. Larry Christenson, author of *Welcome, Holy Spirit* (Minneapolis: Augsburg, 1987, p. 17), observes that no other movement in history has spread so quickly and so extensively.

One of the characteristics of people in the charismatic movement is that they emphasize the gifts of the Spirit. What are these gifts—the charismata? Why are they called charismata? How did this term orig-inate? Are they as essential to the church today as they seem to have been in apostolic times? If not, why not? If they are essential to the life of the church today, why is there occasionally hostility and dis-harmony associated with some of them? Are they dismissed because they are so mysterious and do not lend themselves readily to rational explanation? Is God conveying a message to the church through the charismata whereby the church is enabled to be more effective in communicating the gospel?

Some have wondered whether some of these people are emotionally disturbed. Some critics have even suspected that people who demon-strate the gifts of charismata, particularly the manifestational gifts (see chap. 5), are mentally disoriented. However, such accusations need to be quickly put to rest. Evidence indicates no more emotional disorders among charismatics than in the general population. Substantiating evidence clearly indicates that these people are as normal as any in society. There is no evidence that they are more or less emotionally balanced or unbalanced than the rest of society.

In order to proceed on a solid foundation we need to search God's Word and seek guidance from the Holy Spirit to discern whether there is a sound biblical basis for such charismatic experiences. An emotional experience alone is not sufficient to satisfy our longing for truth and reality. Scripture lends credibility to such experiences. From its words we are able to distinguish what is normative. We will attempt to provide a practical, biblical approach to utilizing the charismata in ways that limit disharmony and disunity in the body of Christ, the church.

What Are Charismata?

In this chapter, we will not consider all the gifts of the Spirit but focus more specifically on one group of gifts called the charismata. The word *charismata* is the plural form of the Greek noun *charisma*, which

is translated "gift." These gifts include the controversial gifts of prophecy, discerning of spirits, and glossolalia or "tongues," as it is commonly
called.

In order to understand the meaning and significance of charismata,
we also need to understand why the Spirit of God gives these gifts to
the church. In studying the context of each group of charismata, we
conclude they were given by the Spirit to equip the body of Christ to
be more effective in its specific function and purpose. The function
and purpose for the church is to proclaim the love of God in Christ
Jesus to the entire world.

How does the history of the church fit into this picture of the charismata? God has always had a people of his own—first Israel, then
also the church. As a seed is buried in the ground and passes through
various stages, first underground and then above ground, so the people
of God also passed and continue to pass through various stages. The
church itself was born on Pentecost and is being led through various
phases to continued growth and maturity.

At first the church was hidden in Israel, the nation through whom
God chose to manifest his plan of salvation. The plan of God became
incarnate with the birth of Jesus Christ in the manger at Bethlehem
and finally manifested itself in power on the first Pentecost and spread
throughout the world.

The purpose of the church from Pentecost onwards always was and
continues to be to witness to the love of God in Christ. The love of
God desires all people to be saved. The Spirit of God was poured out
in various manifestations so that Christians could be effective witnesses
to Jesus Christ, the Savior of the world. The gifts of the Spirit were
given that the Father might be glorified through the Son. "But you
will receive power when the Holy Spirit has come upon you; and you
will be my witnesses in Jerusalem, and in all Judea and Samaria, and
to the ends of the earth" (ACTS 1:8).

This was the initial phase in the life of the church. In the church
the Holy Spirit continues to bring people to the assurance of salvation
in Christ and equip them for service. To enable this process of witnessing
and ministering God's love, the Holy Spirit imparts spiritual gifts. But
the word *gift* is not always used or meant in the same way. The fact
that the word is used in various ways indicates that there are various
gifts. Therefore we need to be specific when we talk about gifts or risk
confusion.

In some passages in the New Testament the word *gift* is used in the sense of a blessing being offered to God. It is intended to convey bringing something of value to God: "So when you are offering your gift at the altar . . . (MATT. 5:23).

Other passages convey the message that the gift is one given by the grace of God in Christ such as the gift of salvation: "Thanks be to God for his indescribable gift!" (2 COR. 9:15).

A gift that is offered to God is called *doron* in the Greek (MATT. 5:23-24; 8:4; 15:5; MARK 7:11; LUKE 21:4; HEB. 5:1; 8:3-4; 9:9; 11:4). The gift of grace from God is usually called *dorea* (MATT. 10:8; ROM. 3:24; 2 COR. 11:7). This demonstrates quite clearly that these gifts are different from the word *charismata*. To lump all gifts together in one large category can create confusion and frustration.

The charismata are revealed to us in specific categories that enable us to determine what our specific gift or gifts might be. Later chapters will look at those categories.

We also need to state that the Holy Spirit itself is the gift or a gift of God's grace. This raises some questions as to whether the Holy Spirit is *the* gift or *a* gift. There are passages that seem to justify both. Jesus said,

> Is there anyone among you who, if your child asks for a fish, will give a snake instead of a fish? Or, if the child asks for an egg, will give a scorpion? If you then, who are evil, know how to give good gifts to your children, how much more will the heavenly Father give the Holy Spirit to those who ask him (LUKE 11:11-13).

Peter, on the day of Pentecost, urged the crowd to gather around to receive what was available to them when he said, "Repent, and be baptized every one of you in the name of Jesus Christ so that your sins may be forgiven; and you will receive the gift of the Holy Spirit" (ACTS 2:38).

The Spirit of God in essence is the gift. Various other gifts and, specifically, the charismata, are manifestations of the Spirit. The Spirit of God is manifested through these gifts as the Spirit ministers to people through people. We will refer to them as office, personality, and manifestational gifts.

In order to explain how the Holy Spirit bestows these gifts through God's grace, we might use the analogy of a river that flows within the banks of a channel. The river makes its way downstream where some of the water flows into smaller irrigation channels. In these channels it proceeds in various ways to water all kinds of living things as it flows out on dry land. As it waters it brings the necessities of life to living organisms. Those organisms grow and bring forth fruit.

We might compare the river to the Holy Spirit. Grace is the channel through which the Spirit flows. The smaller channels might be compared to the charismata that provide the necessities for people in their daily walk with God. These people, after receiving the gifts, bring forth abundant fruit.

Charismata are not gifts to be manipulated. The office and personality gifts seem to be given to us as perpetual enablements for all times and for every circumstance that may arise in the future. The manifestational gifts seem to be given more instantaneously by the Holy Spirit at the specific moment when they are needed to convey the love of God and bring honor to his name. No person can choose to receive the gifts at will, but the Spirit can choose any person to manifest any gift as the Spirit wills. Therefore, anyone who is baptized and empowered by the Spirit is a candidate through whom the Spirit of God may become manifest in some manner through various gifts.

But even in this there seems to be a paradox. To have the Spirit does not mean that we own the Spirit or the gifts we receive. Neither the Spirit of God nor these gifts are possessions to which we can lay ownership. The Spirit of God is not a thing to be obtained so that we can claim a possessive kind of ownership and say the Spirit is "ours." It is the Spirit who, by the grace of God, possesses Christians. This is clarified by John Koenig as he states:

> While the Spirit somehow resides in individual believers, they in no sense have it at their disposal. The Spirit cannot be owned or contained by anyone, not even the corporate body of the church. It is more accurate to say that the Spirit possesses the church (Charismata: God's Gifts for God's People, Philadelphia: Westminster Press, 1978, p. 74).

The actions and manifestations of the Spirit of God cannot be reduced to stereotypes. The Spirit of God is inexhaustible. About the time we think we have arrived, we realize that there is still more. There is always more to the Spirit than any Christian can understand or comprehend. We can never quite arrive at the point where we can say this or that is the specific manner in which the Spirit of God always moves and works. There is what we might call consistent inconsistency.

On the day of Pentecost we read that the disciples "were filled with the Holy Spirit" (ACTS 2:4). But a short time later we read they were filled again (ACTS 4:31). This seems to indicate that they had the Spirit but not indefinitely, consistently, and with totality; therefore they could be filled again. This is in keeping with what Paul admonishes, "Do not get drunk with wine, for that is debauchery; but be filled with the Spirit" (EPH. 5:18).

The Greek verb meaning "be filled" is a second person plural, present, imperative, passive—which infers that we are presently and continually to be filled with the Spirit. The reason seems to be that the Spirit of God is constantly active. In order for there to be a pouring out of the Spirit, there needs to be a pouring in.

Christians never get to the point that they have so much of the Spirit that they are not in need of more of the Spirit's power. If the Spirit has proper access to an individual, the Spirit's goal is not the indwelling of the person as the end result, but rather to be poured out through her or him. So as the Spirit is being poured out through the individual, there is always need for more of the Spirit to be poured in.

From this we see that the Spirit of God comes with a specific reason: to equip God's people for specific purposes. The first purpose is to bring people to the assurance of salvation. The assurance of salvation is not meant to be a gift that becomes an end in itself, but is rather a means to an end. By this we do not mean that after we have come to the assurance of salvation there is nothing left for us to do but sit and wait for a blissful eternity.

This brings us to the second purpose of the Spirit which is to equip Christians for service. Both justification (being forgiven) and sanctification (growing in holiness) are the work of the Spirit of God. In some respects justification and sanctification are one and the same, yet they are separate. It is for sanctification—or effective "fruit bearing"— that the Spirit of God distributes the gifts called charismata.

A family of words is centered around the Greek root *char*. The word for "joy" is *chara*. The word for "rejoicing" is *chairo*. The word for "thanksgiving" is *eucharista* or *eucharisteo* from which we get our English word "eucharist." We also get the word "grace" from *charis*. Then from the word "grace" (*charis*) we get the word "gift" (*charisma*), "bestowing" (*charizomai*) or the plural "gifts" (*charismata*).

It is significant that joy, rejoicing, bestowing, thanksgiving, grace, and gifts all trace themselves to the same root. It is also significant that all these words are related to joy or thanksgiving. We can conclude that by grace (*charis*) God bestows gifts (*charismata*) to his people so they can be effective in ministry. This produces joy (*chara*) and praise or thanksgiving (*eucharista*) to God.

It is fascinating to examine the circumstances that encouraged joy and rejoicing in the New Testament. As Christians experienced the grace of God in their lives there was great rejoicing (ACTS 8:39). The early believers rejoiced when people came to believe in Christ for the assurance of their salvation. As they allowed the grace of God free access to their lives, they experienced joy and thanksgiving in their lives:

> Then in his joy he goes and sells all that he has and buys that field (MATT. 13:44).

> He brought them up into the house and set food before them; and he and his entire household rejoiced that he had become a believer in God (ACTS 16:34).

> Just so, I tell you, there is joy in the presence of the angels of God over one sinner who repents (LUKE 15:10).

There are dozens of other examples of rejoicing. The disciples were glad and rejoiced when they saw the Lord after his resurrection (JOHN 20:19-20). They also rejoiced as they gathered together for their eucharistic meal which was a continuation of fellowship with the risen Christ (ACTS 2:46). They also rejoiced in the power that was manifest in the very name of Jesus in the ministry of exorcisms (LUKE 10:17) and healing miracles (ACTS 3:6-8; 4:29-30; 5:15-16). They not only rejoiced in their fellowship with Christ, but also in their fellowship with each other through Christ (ROM. 15:7-13). They rejoiced in the fact that the Spirit of God transformed hearers into believers in Christ:

> I was overjoyed when some of the friends arrived and testified to your faithfulness to the truth, namely how you walk in the

truth. I have no greater joy than this, to hear that my children are walking in the truth (3 JOHN 3-4).

Christians could even find joy in their trials and sufferings (1 PET. 4:13). It may be hard for the rational mind to be able to understand and comprehend the deeper meaning of that joy. How is it possible to rejoice in suffering? What is the relationship between this family of words— eucharist, grace, joy, thanksgiving, and gifts—and suffering gladly for Christ? This brings us to the next section.

Grace, Rejoicing, and Charismata

Paul, in writing to the Corinthians, states that "those who are un-spiritual do not receive the gifts of God's Spirit, for they are foolishness to them" (1 COR. 2:14). Initially, that seems like a rather arrogant, exclusive statement uttered by someone reacting against the rational. But more likely it is saying that the spiritually experienced will be able to appreciate or comprehend the things of the Spirit. Martin Luther, in his commentary on Romans, says:

> Between grace and gift there is this difference. Grace means properly God's favor, or the good-will God bears us, by which He is disposed to give us Christ and to pour into us the Holy Ghost, with His gifts. This is clear from chapter 5, where he speaks of "the grace and gift in Christ." The gifts and the Spirit increase in us every day, though they are not yet perfect, and there remain in us the evil lust and sin that war against the Spirit, as Paul says in Romans 7 and Galatians 5, and the quarrel between the seed of the woman and the seed of the serpent is foretold in Genesis 3. Nevertheless, grace does so much that we are accounted wholly righteous before God. For His grace is not divided or broken up, as are the gifts, but it takes us entirely into favor, for the sake of Christ our Intercessor and Mediator, and because of that the gifts are begun in us (*Commentary on the Epistle to the Romans*, Grand Rapids: Zondervan, 1976, p. xiv).

By now we are motivated enough to probe deeper into things of the Spirit and especially the charismata. Furthermore we long to know how the charismata are related to grace, joy, and thanksgiving.

In studying these words we have noted a relationship between grace (charis), gifts (charismata), joy (chara), and thanksgiving (eucharista) since they are all related to the same root (char).

This relationship manifests itself in various ways in our Christian experience. Individuals who suddenly experience the love of God in Christ through forgiveness cannot help but rejoice. In gratitude they are moved to serve the Lord, and in order to serve effectively, they long for gifts that will enable them to do that. Joy is often one of the first manifestations after the initial touch of the Spirit of God in a person's life. Remember the eunuch who went on his way rejoicing (ACTS 8:39).

The joy is so overwhelming that those with a newfound faith desire to share their blessing with everyone who comes their way. This may often be with those who have not experienced this grace, and to them such excitement may seem fanatical, excessive, and perhaps even offensive. The unsaved or inexperienced are unable to understand how anyone can be so enthusiastic about his or her faith. Their only conclusion is that such people must be emotionally disturbed. In one sense, this may be a correct evaluation.

Their emotions are disturbed with an inner touch of the Spirit of God such as they have never experienced before. They are so delighted that they long to share this newfound joy with others. In their zeal and joy they sometimes do more harm than good. Therefore, proper teaching and orientation is necessary so that their experience and overzealousness do not become sources of disharmony and disunity.

We are increasingly more aware that as the grace of God moves about in the lives of people, transformations take place that move beyond the boundaries of the rational. It becomes apparent that true joy cannot be understood or experienced apart from grace. Neither can charismata be received or experienced apart from grace.

True joy is a deep human experience. It is more than a passing fancy or momentary frill. True joy has looked into the deepest recesses of life for meaning and fulfillment. True joy looks beyond the moment to the wider reality of time and eternity. True joy is focused on a reality that keeps it going. Scripture informs us about the basis for this joy when we read that the fruit of the Spirit is love, joy, and many other positive attributes (GAL. 5:22-23).

It is important for us to understand joy as it is related to other characteristics of the Christian life. Joy is related to charismata, and these gifts called charismata cannot be studied independent of their family ties. We need to look at grace, joy, thanksgiving, and all gifts in their relationship to each other. Then we are able to understand why Paul can urge people to rejoice in suffering because the Holy Spirit within them will use such trials to produce endurance, character, and hope (ROM. 5:1-5).

To some outsiders, the Christian faith may seem somewhat masochistic. Historical sources record for us the joyful responses of people dying for the sake of Christ. The basis for such joyful response, even in the face of death, is apparently the grace of God in Christ that manifests itself in joy (*chara*), gifts (*charismata*), and thanksgiving (*eucharista*).

The word *charisma* appears seventeen times in the New Testament (ROM. 1:11; 5:15, 16; 6:23; 11:29; 12:6; 1 COR. 1:7; 7:7; 12:4, 9, 28, 30-31; 2 COR. 1:11; 1 TIM. 4:14; 2 TIM. 1:6; 1 PET. 4:10). Paul uses the word *charisma* with both present and future connotations. Notice this passage: "For the wages of sin is death, but the free gift (*charisma*) of God is eternal life in Christ Jesus our Lord" (ROM. 6:23). Here charisma is used with a connotation of something that comes to us sometime in the future. But in most other passages charisma is used within the present context as when Paul says, "For I am longing to see you so that I may share with you some spiritual gift (*charisma*) to strengthen you" (ROM. 1:11). The present tense indicates that it is a gift for the present as well as the future.

The charismata are gifts that come to Christians without any merit or effort on their part. Some charismata are given to many people and others are given with more specificity. The charismata of encouragement, release, and healing seem to fall into a natural grouping. As Koenig says,

> We can, without being judgmental, call them gifts passively received. They come like nourishment, to those whose lives need renewing. At the time of their reception these charismata do not contain within themselves specific directives for ministry. But there are other charismata, most of them in fact, which do exactly that (*Charismata: God's Gifts for God's People*, Philadelphia: Westminster Press, 1978, p. 99).

The point here is that charismata are given to nourish and to enable ministry. The intent is that they be used generously for the benefit of the body of Christ and the world. Paul states, "To each is given the manifestation of the Spirit for the common good" (1 COR. 12:7 RSV).

All that we have said previously indicates that the gifts come to us by the grace of God. They are made available to us so that we might share them with the rest of God's people. Nevertheless we need to remind ourselves and others that the Spirit of God provides opportunities and the enabling, but never compels a person to act. Once again this may seem like a paradox. All is of grace, but grace does not preclude an act of the will as Paul states, "Work out your own salvation with fear and trembling; for it is God who is at work in you, enabling you both to will and to work for his good pleasure" (PHIL. 2:12-13).

Charismata are not replacements for human initiative. We need to refer to them as gifts of God's grace, promises, enablings, or calls for ministry. But, ultimately, they involve the will of a humble servant who moves forward with whatever gifts he or she has been given, putting them into practice in the church and in the world. Using gifts is a working out or demonstration of the faith that is within.

To put a gift into practice in a wrong or harmful manner is simply to repeat the mistakes of the Corinthians that caused division and disharmony in the body of Christ. This is apparent from such passages as, "If I speak in the tongues of mortals and of angels, but do not have love, I am a noisy gong or a clanging cymbal" (1 COR. 13:1-2).

It is quickly apparent that wrong, proud, or arrogant utilization of the charismata does not bring the blessings God intended. The purpose of the charismata in the Christian congregation is to maximize the potential for harmony and mutual ministry for the benefit of all to the glory of God in Christ. The very fact that we are to use our gifts for the benefit of all in the body of Christ is necessary because everyone does not have every gift. If everyone had every gift all the time, we would be totally self-sufficient.

The New Testament's qualifying phrases, as we will study later, demonstrate that we cannot be self-sufficient. Rather, we need others in the body of Christ in order to experience wholeness or completeness. Love, right priorities, and proper order are required. These are elaborated by Paul in 1 Corinthians 13 and 14.

Living in Joyful Expectation

Christians have every reason to live expectantly because God's Word informs us that "Jesus Christ is the same yesterday and today and forever"

(HEB. 13:8). Jesus is alive and is able to minister to us as he ministered to people in the past. He has not changed nor has his desire to touch people in their greatest need, whatever that may be. So we can look to him with the greatest of expectation and anticipation in all our needs.

We need to determine how to apply and appropriate all the gifts that are ours in Christ in a proper manner so that we do not fall prey to deception or error. Not everyone agrees that there is something to appropriate. Occasionally in the past and present, arguments have been raised stating that the charismata are no longer relevant for our day. Merrill Unger, one such person, states:

> But as credentials of an apostle and as confirmation of the
> Gospel, these miraculous charismata passed away after the
> apostolic period, when apostles no longer existed and the
> Christian faith no longer needed such outward signs to confirm
> it. This important fact is not only intimated by Scripture but
> well attested by church history (The Baptism of the Holy Spirit,
> Chicago: Moody Press, 1974, p. 139).

Unger argues that the miraculous gifts were given to establish credentials for the apostles and passed away when the apostles died.

J. R. Pridie also accepted this same line of thought:

> The charismatic gifts have usually been considered as extra-
> ordinary activities of the Holy Spirit connected exclusively
> with the first age of the church's life. Their purpose has been
> thought to be simply evidential of her mission and character.
> They were her credentials and having established her claims,
> were not looked for in the later developments of her history
> (The Spiritual Gifts, London: Robert Scott).

More research has been done in recent years and there is increasing substantiating evidence that the charismata have not vanished but are still relevant and in practice. There is no substantiating evidence for us to believe that the charismata are not relevant for our day. Recent research points to historical evidence that gifts continued in use in the early church and even to the present. C. P. Wagner writes:

> In the second century both Justin Martyr and Irenaeus
> acknowledged that the miraculous gifts were in operation in

the church. In the third century, Hippolytus makes reference to one of his writings, "On Charismatic Gifts," but the essay has never been located. In the same century, Tertullian observed with approval the exercise of spiritual gifts, and then himself converted to Montanism, a kind of third-century charismatic movement which was declared heretical by many of the mainline Christians. Bishop Hilary of the fourth century spoke of the exercise of the gifts with favor, as did John Chrysostom. The great theologian of the fifth century, Augustine, is interpreted as supporting both those who say the gifts blinked off and those who say they continued. However, James King has discovered that Augustine "completely reversed his views on Miracles. Originally he disputed their continuance into his day. He later taught their present validity and claimed to be an eyewitness to some miracles."

Thomas Aquinas, in the thirteenth century, considered the charismatic gifts as essential to the church, although he did not address the matter of whether they actually had continued after the apostolic age (*Your Spiritual Gifts*, Ventura, Calif.: GL Publications, 1985, Preface, pp. 24-25).

More evidence points to the tremendous blessings of taking the charismata seriously and appropriating them to minister more effectively for the benefit of all. In light of such blessings it appears to be a tragic mistake for us to be selective in accepting some gifts that may not be as controversial and rejecting others that may not seem to fit into our framework of rational thinking.

It is interesting to read about past experiences of saints as they relate their charismatic experiences. John Wesley wrote:

We were present at our love feast in Fetter Lane with about sixty of our brethren. About three in the morning as we were continuing instant in prayer, the power of God came mightily upon us, insomuch that many cried out for exceeding joy, and many fell to the ground. As soon as we recovered a little from the awe and amazement at this presence of His majesty we broke out with one voice, "We praise thee, O God, we acknowledge thee to be Lord" (*The Journal* 1 [January 1739]: 160).

Luther in his famous hymn of the Reformation, "A Mighty Fortress," wrote:

> The Word they shall allow to stand,
> Nor any thanks have for it;
> He is with us, of our right hand,
> With the gifts of His Spirit. (*Mit seinem Geist und Gaben*,
> author translation).

The evidence indicates that the charismata continued to be in existence and practiced throughout the life of the church. Jesus is "the same yesterday and today and forever." Therefore, there is good reason for us to become informed on proper practice of these gifts. To disregard or downgrade these gifts of the Spirit may be more serious than we would like to admit.

When I was in seminary in 1957, we were taught that only one sin is unforgivable, and that is the sin against the Holy Spirit, speaking against or blaspheming against the Holy Spirit (MATT. 12:31, MARK 3:28-29, LUKE 12:10). In reference to this warning, W. C. Allen writes:

> The meaning seems to be: "You have taken sides against Me in the war against Satan. In so doing you have committed an unpardonable sin, because in charging Me with being an agent of Satan you have hardened yourselves against a revelation of God's Spirit working in me" (*The International Critical Commentary*, Edinburgh: T and T Clark, 1955, p. 136).

While there may be some controversy about what specific sin is meant, there is still only one sin the New Testament says is unforgivable and that is the sin against the Holy Spirit. Therefore we need to be extremely cautious and serious about how we deal with that which is of the Spirit of God.

In my research I have found no sound and convincing arguments to discontinue to live in the expectancy of all that God has to offer to us through the charismata. As I have consulted with bishops and church leaders, the word has consistently been one of encouragement to pursue all that is available to us from the Spirit of God without hesitancy.

There seems to be overwhelming scriptural support in favor of openness and practice of these gifts, the charismata. Paul in writing to the

Romans says, "For the gifts (*charismata*) and the calling of God are irrevocable" (ROM. 11:29). Also, Jesus himself promises, "The one who believes in me . . . will do greater works than these, because I am going to the Father" (JOHN 14:12).

In light of these and other passages in Scripture it seems that the spiritual gifts, specifically the charismata, which have their source in the Lord and to which the early disciples gave testimony, are not revocable but are as relevant as Christ himself. For the gifts come from the Spirit, and the Spirit is the Spirit of Christ himself, as we read, "But you are not in the flesh; you are in the Spirit, since the Spirit of God dwells in you. Anyone who does not have the Spirit of Christ does not belong to him" (ROM. 8:9).

With assurances from Scripture and testimony from many Christian leaders, we move forward boldly, yet humbly and cautiously, in expectation of all that there is for us in the Spirit and through the Spirit. Those of us who are part of the charismatic movement do not in any way desire to give the impression that we have all the answers. We are searching and need to examine all the evidence that is placed before us.

We need to emphasize the fact that the gift which is the Holy Spirit comes to us in entirety, at one time. This means that the Holy Spirit does not come to us in fragmented form a little at a time. Nevertheless, because we have all of the Spirit of God does not necessarily mean that the Spirit has all of us. For this reason we need to be open continuously to the infilling of the Spirit of God so that it may both pour itself into us and out to others at the same time.

I believe this flow of the Holy Spirit begins with the Sacrament of Holy Baptism where the Spirit is initially bestowed. "Repent, and be baptized every one of you in the name of Jesus Christ so that your sins may be forgiven; and you will receive the gift of the Holy Spirit" (ACTS 2:38). At baptism we receive all of the Spirit of God. But this does not mean that all of the Spirit of God is appropriated simply because we are baptized. The filling and outpouring of the Spirit of God is a constant, ongoing process as can be understood from Paul's words in Ephesians, "Be filled with the Spirit" (EPH. 5:18).

The gifts of the Spirit have their specific purposes. Baptized with the gift and empowered with the gifts, Christians are ready for their calling in the world. Paul understands the work of the Spirit to be the honoring of Jesus Christ as Lord and Savior. Therefore, it is not surprising that he understands the work of the spiritually gifted to be that of service to the body of Christ for Christ's sake, using the charismata. This is revealed to us as he elaborates rather extensively on things of the Spirit, and at the conclusion he asks,

> What then are we to say about these things? If God is for us, who is against us? He who did not withhold his own Son, but gave him up for all of us, will he not with him also give [the Greek word is *charisetai* which means "to bestow a gracious gift"] us everything else (ROM. 8:31-32).

The impression given from this passage is that Paul readily anticipated other charismata to be given to the body of Christ in the future.

We find the same true in 1 Corinthians where he states with an indication of expectancy, "So that you are not lacking in any spiritual gift as you wait for the revealing of our Lord Jesus Christ. He will also strengthen you to the end" (1 COR. 1:7-8).

This gives us reason to believe that the charismata are given in a series of ongoing revelations for specific situations and circumstances that have a need for specific gifts. Each additional revelation is unique in its own way and capable of standing by itself, yet also complementing and contributing to the whole. Furthermore, when seen in the light of such ongoing revelation, there is order and specificity without confusion.

Some textual evidence exists for this conclusion. Most sources agree that Corinthians was written by Paul in about A.D. 53–57, that Romans was written next in about A.D. 54–58, and that Ephesians was written in A.D. 61–70. While there is some controversy over Pauline authorship of Ephesians, it does not detract from the idea that we have a series of revelations in these books given at different times and under different situations and circumstances.

After examining all these texts closely, we can see that in the charismata are different categories or sets of gifts. It does not seem to be good scholarship to lump all the charismata together into one category. Such phrases as "some," "differ," "to each," and "for everyone" in the texts on charismata seem to warrant a separate consideration for each group in its specific setting, time, place, and purpose.

Each text has its own way to deal with the specific gifts mentioned and has distinct parameters for whom and to whom the gifts are directed. Ignoring these simple details causes confusion that may readily lead to suspicion and disharmony in a given congregation. To demonstrate the uniqueness of each text, let us point out the characteristics in its setting that make the text unique. We will examine them in the light of the whole, much as one is able to look back at prophetic words that related to Jesus in the light of their fulfillment. We will see quite clearly the manner in which they in their uniqueness add to the whole, yet fit together "decently and in order" (1 COR. 14:40).

QUESTIONS FOR DISCUSSION OR REFLECTION

1. Why are some people inclined to give the impression they own the gifts that the Holy Spirit has given them? In what ways is this a detriment to the Christian church?

2. In Greek the words for joy, rejoicing, eucharist, and thanksgiving all come from the same root as charismata (gifts). In what way does this bring enlightenment to better understand the charismata?

3. Some scholars have said that the more miraculous gifts were only present and necessary during the early days of the church, then they passed out of existence; others say they continue to the present. What is your opinion and what biblical basis do you have for your conclusion?

PART TWO

Specific
Categories of
Charismata

CHAPTER 3

Office Gifts

EPHESIANS 4:11-12

In order to know more about the office gifts mentioned in Ephesians 4:11-12, we need to look at the reason they are given as stated in verse 12: "to equip the saints for the work of ministry, for building up the body of Christ."

First we will look at what might be included in ministry. The call to minister is extended to all who belong to the universal priesthood of believers—to all Christians. On the other hand, the official call to ministry (we might say ordained ministry) is given to "some," as we discover in this Ephesians text.

In the Old Testament only the divinely appointed high priest was permitted to enter the holy of holies in order by sacrifice and prayer to make intercession between God and the people. In the New Testament through the atonement of Christ this is changed so that all Christians have the privilege to approach God's throne of grace. Paul consistently emphasizes this in such passages as:

Through whom we have obtained access to this grace in which we stand (ROM. 5:2).

So he came and proclaimed peace to you who were far off and peace to those who were near; for through him both of us have access in one Spirit to the Father (EPH. 2:17-18).

This was in accordance with the eternal purpose that he has carried out in Christ Jesus our Lord, in whom we have access to God in boldness and confidence through faith in him (EPH. 3:11-12).

This New Testament priesthood of all believers is both a privilege and a duty. It is a privilege because it affords us direct access to God in prayer; it is a duty because it obligates us to share, by our words and deeds, the love of God in Christ who made it possible. As priests, Christians are given the right and the duty to share the message of the gospel with all people.

But there is another aspect that is specifically applicable to Ephesians 4:11, "The gifts he gave were that some would be . . ." Article XIV of the Augsburg Confession, a Lutheran confessional document, speaks specifically to this subject when it addresses the topic of "Ecclesiastical Order," stating that public administration of the means of grace, that is, the Word and sacraments, in the individual congregation "ought to be allowed no one unless he be *rightly called.*"

Because the members of the body of Christ cannot maintain a proper relationship with Jesus Christ apart from the means of grace, and because they cannot carry out their specific calling to minister without the administration of the means of grace, the church needs an office of public administration for the means of grace: the pastor or ordained minister.

The office of public administration of the means of grace is not merely a product of social expediency; it is based upon an explicit divine calling. God not only gives the church individuals who are especially called for the administration of the office of pastor, but people with other gifts as well, as we read,

> The gifts he gave were that some would be apostles, some prophets, some evangelists, some pastors and teachers, to equip the saints for the work of ministry, for building up the body of Christ (EPH. 4:11-12).

The Holy Spirit calls them through the congregation, and the congregation calls them to specific offices. This appears to be confirmed in such a passage as: "Keep watch over yourselves and over all the flock, of which the Holy Spirit has made you overseers, to shepherd the church of God that he obtained with the blood of his own Son" (ACTS 20:28).

In this context we can consider the unique aspects of the text in Ephesians 4:11-12. As stated earlier, this likely was the last of the charismata texts to be written either by Paul or possibly by one of his students. Although the word *charisma* does not appear in the Ephesians account, the concept of special gifts from the risen Christ is clearly implied. The *charis* (grace) of God in Ephesians 3:2, 7 manifests itself in various *charismata* in 4:7.

It was the ascended Christ who "gave gifts to his people" (EPH. 4:8). It is the ascended Christ who has all gifts and who dispenses his abundance to us. It is the gift of grace that makes the other gifts possible to Christians. In *The International Critical Commentary*, T. K. Abbott states that the specific words chosen by the author in the text are not mistakes but were carefully selected so that the "gifts" (*edoken*) in Ephesians 4:11 are meant to harmonize with "he gave gifts" (*edoken domata*) in 4:8. Abbott says it is as if the author said, "And the gifts He gave were some as apostles, others as prophets, others as evangelists and others as pastors and teachers" ("Epistles to the Ephesians and the Colossians," *The International Critical Commentary*, New York: Charles Scribner and Sons, 1916, p. 117).

The gifts in this text are not activities or things, but specific individuals. The writer lists apostles, prophets, evangelists, pastors, and teachers as Christ's gifts (*domata*) to the church, but he does not apply the word *gift* (*charismata*) to people, not even to those who are seen or called to be leaders or office holders in the church. The nearest Paul comes to equating the two is this passage in 1 Corinthians:

> And God has appointed in the church first apostles, second prophets, third teachers, then deeds of power, then gifts (*charismata*) of healing, forms of assistance, forms of leadership, various kinds of tongues (1 COR. 12:28).

All of this seems to indicate that there is a reason the writer refrains from using the word (*charismata*) for people. John Koenig states:

> Technically, only the last five [activities] can be called charismata [1 COR. 12:9-10]. Apparently Paul wants to make sure that his readers understand the difference between people and spiritual gifts that are granted to them. The gift is not the person; therefore no one can glory in it as if it were a personal

accomplishment, a deserved payment for outstanding piety or
services rendered (*Charismata: God's Gifts for God's People*,
Philadelphia: Westminster Press, 1978, p. 103).

This Ephesians text contains elements not found in any of the other
charismata texts. First, Ephesians speaks of "some" (*men-de*). This is a
clear indication of limitation. One source states that there is

> a particle serving to indicate that the term or clause with
> which it is used stands distinguished from another, usually in
> the sequel, and then mostly with (*de*)—meaning "to one this,
> to another that" (*A Greek English Lexicon of the New Testament*,
> Chicago: University of Chicago Press, 1957, p. 504).

It is a great mistake in interpretation to ignore this indication of
limitation and assume that these gifts are for all in the body of Christ,
thereby lumping them in with the other charismata mentioned in 1
Corinthians, Romans, and 1 Peter. Rather, these are gifts that call a
specific individual to a specific office or type of ministry. This characteristic is not evident in the other categories of gifts. Therefore, these
gifts in the Ephesians account are unique. In context we determine
that these are gifts of an official nature. Specific individuals are called
to specific offices or ministries.

The purpose of each of these office gifts is spelled out quite syste-
matically "to (*pros*) equip the saints for (*eis*) the work of ministry, for
(*eis*) building up the body of Christ" (EPH. 4:12). This is a direct statement
to the church.

The way the church most often has done its ministry in our generation—with the pastor in charge, responsible for most of the ministry
of the church—is not the way it was or is intended. Rather the calling
of the office gift is quite specific "to equip the saints, for the work of
ministry, for building up the body of Christ" (EPH. 4:12). The office gifts
are bestowed so that the entire body might be enabled to minister
effectively in Christ Jesus.

The individuals who are called to these specific offices or ministry
are not called to do the ministry themselves. The specifics of this text
demonstrate the way the work (*diakonia*) of the kingdom is to be done.
These individuals who are called by the Spirit of God to these offices

are called to equip the saints, to enable God's people to minister, to
build up or advance the body of Christ.

In the same respect each specific office of the five mentioned is
apparently a different calling in the body of Christ. Each specific office
gift has a different approach to the process of equipping saints to minister
the love of God in Christ. Each specific office is still relevant, functional, and essential to the well-being of the church for our day. Some
of these offices may be less visible in the church today due to lack of
understanding and expectation. This does not mean that such individuals or ministries did not exist or do not exist today in spite of the
lack of expectation on the part of the church.

Markus Barth has written concerning this viewpoint:

> The author of this epistle did not anticipate that the inspired
> and enthusiastic ministry was to be absorbed by, and
> "disappear" into, offices and officers bare of the Holy Spirit
> and restful of any reference to spiritual things. Ephesians 4
> does not contain the faintest hint that the charismatic
> character of all church ministries was restricted to a certain
> period of church history and was later to die out (*Ephesians 4–
> 6*, Garden City, N.Y.: Doubleday & Co., 1974, p. 437).

Historical figures such as Luther, Calvin, Knox, Zwingli, Spurgeon,
Benedict of Nursia, Francis of Assisi, the Swedish seer Birgitta, and
many others could readily fit the scriptural characteristics of an apostolic
or prophetic ministry. These people had a specific calling and a gift to
see through and beyond circumstances. In the same manner they exuded
an authority that motivated respect from many who followed them. It
was not a self-proclaimed authority, but one that originated from the
Spirit of God and was confirmed by a body of believers. All this was
not accomplished by them through active campaigning, but by divine
appointment and confirmation by a congregation of believers.

The Spirit of God is still calling individuals to these specific offices
in order that the saints might be properly equipped for the work of
ministry—for building up the body of Christ. What are the specific
characteristics of each office or ministry? How are they defined and
explained in the Scriptures?

Apostles

The first office gift mentioned in Ephesians 4:11 and 1 Corinthians 12:28 is that of apostle. It is the highest office and calling in the body of Christ. It gets preferential treatment in both texts. This might well be the reason that the author stated earlier in his letter to the Ephesians:

> So then you are no longer strangers and aliens, but you are citizens with the saints and also members of the household of God, built upon the foundation of the apostles and prophets, Christ Jesus himself as the cornerstone. In him the whole structure is joined together and grows into a holy temple in the Lord; in whom you also are built together spiritually into a dwelling place for God (EPH. 2:19-20).

This passage emphasizes the ongoing nature of the process of building a dwelling place for God. It has Christ Jesus as the cornerstone, but it is built upon the foundation of apostles and prophets. As Christ continues to be the functional cornerstone, so the foundational process of apostles and prophets continues functional. There is no indication that this process is to be terminated, much as we do not terminate "salvation by grace through faith" by eliminating or ignoring the passage that we are saved by grace and not by works (EPH. 2:8).

To define the concept of "apostle" is difficult. Most sources generalize when it comes to the office of the apostle. A frequent conclusion is that the office passed out of existence with the original apostles. Nevertheless, that understanding does not satisfy our longing to discover if there is some way that this office may be applied to us in our day.

New Testament tradition says that apostles were the individuals to whom the risen Lord appeared and who were commissioned by him as emissaries. But such a general interpretation does leave some unanswered questions. It also leaves the door open for additional interpretation. Barth states:

> The titles "apostle" and "prophet" occur in the NT with both wide and narrow meanings. Sometimes the term "apostle" is filled with connotations of special election and authority; in these cases it is restricted to the twelve disciples of Jesus and

Paul. On other occasions it is used in a wider sense: every witness of the resurrected Christ and anyone delegated by a church for mission work can bear the same title. (MATT. 10:1-5; GAL.1:1, 17, 19; 1 COR. 9:1-2; 15:7; 2 COR. 8:23) (*Ephesians 4–6*, Garden City, N.Y.: Doubleday & Co., 1974, p. 314).

It is interesting to notice that The Living Bible frequently uses "missionary" for the word *apostle*. J. B. Phillips in The New Testament in Modern English uses "messenger" for the word *apostle* in this Ephesians passage.

Some biblical evidence does support the continuity of apostolic ministry. The original twelve apostles have a unique place in history. We recognize the honor that will be theirs in heaven as is described in Rev. 21:14. But this general interpretation leaves many questions unanswered. It does not seem logical that some of the office gifts should be left intact while others be discontinued unless it is specifically stated in the text or context. It is interesting to note that others besides the Twelve were referred to as apostles, including Jesus himself. C. P. Wagner writes:

The biblical evidence strongly supports the continuity of the gift of apostle. The original 12 apostles have a unique place in Christian history and they will be commemorated permanently in the New Jerusalem (see Rev. 21:14), but they were not the only apostles. First Corinthians 15 mentions that after the resurrection Jesus appeared to "the twelve" and then also to "all the apostles," indicating that there were apostles other than the twelve (1 COR. 15:5, 7). Furthermore the warnings against "false apostles" would be nonsense if apostles were limited to the twelve (see 2 COR. 11:13; REV. 2:2).

Several, other than the Twelve, are mentioned by name as apostles. They include Matthias (see ACTS 1:26), Paul (see ROM. 1:1), Barnabas (see ACTS 14:14) Andronicus and Junias (see ROM. 16:7), Timothy and Silas (see 1 Thess. 2:6). Through the ages as well as today, many of God's gifted servants have been and are true apostles (*Your Spiritual Gifts*, Ventura, Calif.: GL Publications, 1985, pp. 207–208).

Evidence exists of an ongoing indefinite process as it relates to apostolic ministry. We can come to some conclusions that enable us to define this ministry a bit more specifically. K. H. Rengstorf provides five uses of the word *apostle* in the New Testament:

a. It always denotes a man who is sent, and sent with full authority.

b. Here *apostolos* is simply a rendering of a legal term in its purely legal sense of one who is lawfully charged to represent the person and cause of another.

c. Like *shaliah*, *apostolos* denotes the "commissioned representative of a congregation."

d. Finally, *apostoloi* is a comprehensive term for "bearers of the NT message." The name is first borne by the circle of twelve, i.e., the original apostles (including Matthias brought in as a replacement in Acts 1:26; cf. *oi—dodeka*, 1 Cor. 15:5). Their sending by Jesus is presupposed. Yet the name is also applied to the first Christian missionaries or their most prominent representatives, including some who did not belong to the wider groups of disciples.

e. In Heb. 3:1 Jesus Himself is called *ho apostolos kai archiereus tes homologias emon*. Here the only possible meaning of *apostolos* is that in Jesus there has taken place the definitive revelation of God by God Himself (1:2) (*Theological Dictionary of the New Testament*, vol. 1, Grand Rapids: Wm. B. Eerdmans, 1982, pp. 421–24).

In light of the above discussion, it may be unwise and confusing to refer to an apostolic office. Instead, it may be wiser and more orderly to refer to this gift as an apostolic ministry. Doing so takes the attention away from the person and places it on the gift and ministry itself. We can, therefore, be a bit more specific about this gift of apostolic ministry.

The apostolic ministry appears to be one where an individual is commissioned by a body of believers—vested with authority and power—to proclaim the gospel of Jesus Christ. This could include what is meant by the word *missionary* but also extend beyond those parameters to include others commissioned to positions of leadership by the body of Christ to proclaim the gospel. This could feasibly include the office of bishop or other specific designated places of leadership that include the proclamation of the gospel of Jesus Christ.

The sequential order expressed in Matthew 10:1-2 implies that before individuals could be considered to be apostles, they needed first to demonstrate faithful discipleship. The evidence of their calling to apostleship was confirmed in what was manifested in their ministry. A true apostle demonstrated consistent, faithful, loving, patient, and dedicated ministry. The apostle's ministry often consisted of manifestations of signs, wonders, and mighty works (2 COR. 12:12).

There are individuals whom the Lord has called to this specific calling of apostolic ministry. The specific calling of apostolic ministry is to proclaim the gospel and provide strong dedicated leadership to the body of Christ. Such leadership is firmly grounded in the lordship of Jesus Christ and faithfulness to the Word of God.

This apostolic ministry is vested with authority by divine calling that also enables and provides stability to the other ministries to function in "equipping the saints for the work of ministry, for building up the body of Christ" (EPH. 4:12). These individuals do not have to campaign for the office in order to be recognized. They are individuals who are readily recognized as ones upon whom the anointing of God has fallen for such apostolic ministry. Furthermore, they also have the respect and support of God's people through whom comes the confirmation and commissioning of such apostolic ministry.

Prophet

The next office gift is that of a prophet. Paul seems to give some preference to prophecy as essential to the body of Christ (1 COR. 14:1). The writers of the Old Testament also recognized the necessity of the prophetic gift and office: "Where there is no prophecy, the people cast off restraint" (PROV. 29:18).

Throughout the Old Testament God provided direction to his people in various ways. God had many ways to communicate to his people, but one of the means for such direction was through the prophets.

The prophetic activity in the Old Testament was probably greatest during the time of the judges and kings of Israel, beginning with Samuel. The prophet was known as a seer. The prophets spoke as individuals to whom the Lord had imparted a message for his people. In other cases they were divinely chosen representatives, and in some instances they were set apart for a lifetime of prophetic ministry.

John F. Walwoord says of Old Testament prophets:

> The quality which distinguished all true prophets from other
> men was their office of speaking for God. Their message was
> not necessarily prophetic in the sense of speaking of future
> events otherwise unknown. Often the prophets preached the
> past, reminding of God's dealings with them. Their message
> was frequently that of specific guidance in the midst of crisis,
> as in the case of Isaiah to Hezekiah when Jerusalem was
> surrounded. Many times their message was one of warning of
> judgement to come for sin. Exhortation was given to worship
> God and obey Him. The prophets because of their sacred office
> were national leaders, patriots, and reformers; they were the
> representatives of God, His mouthpiece of revelation whatever
> the subject. Their lives and ministries did much to shape the
> history of God's people through the Old Testament period (*The
> Holy Spirit*, Grand Rapids: Zondervan, 1969, p. 49).

In the prophecy of Joel, written sometime after the Babylonian exile,
God vows:

> Then afterward I will pour out my spirit on all flesh; your sons
> and your daughters shall prophesy, your old men shall dream
> dreams, and your young men shall see visions. Even on the
> male and female slaves, in those days, I will pour out my spirit
> (JOEL 2:28).

Koenig says:

> The word of the Lord seems to resonate with Moses' wish that
> all God's people might become prophets (NUM. 11:29). Students
> of the New Testament will recall that it is this text from Joel
> which forms the center of Peter's Pentecost sermon in Acts
> 2:16ff. Thus, particularly in the later writings of the Old
> Testament, prophets begin to envision the messianic age as an
> era when spiritual gifts heretofore bestowed upon only a few
> individuals will be poured out upon the whole nation of Israel
> (*Charismata: God's Gifts for God's People*, Philadelphia:
> Westminster Press, 1978, p. 35).

The New Testament prophet was similar in many ways. The differences in many respects are hard to distinguish. This in itself can bring confusion about the prophetic gift mentioned in Ephesians 4. Walwoord defines the New Testament prophet in this way:

> The New Testament prophet partook of some of the characteristics of the Old Testament prophet. Both spoke for God; both warned of judgment upon sin; both delivered their message as from God; both dealt with contemporaneous events as well as predicted events of the future. The Old Testament prophet, however, often had the character of a national leader, reformer, or patriot, and delivered his message normally to Israel. The New Testament prophet has no national characteristics; his message is individual and personal; it revealed the will of God which otherwise might have been unknown, meeting the need which later was to be filled by the written New Testament (*The Holy Spirit*, Grand Rapids: Zondervan, 1969, p. 49).

Barth makes this distinction:

> NT prophets did not claim to have stood in God's council; some, as the seer John on Patmos, may have been given visions, but not all of them claimed them. A political or cultic role was possible but not indispensable for them. Their special charisma appears not only to have been in making predictions of the immediate future—as in the case of Agabus (ACTS 11:28)—but above all in applying the gospel to specific contemporary circumstances (*Ephesians 4–6*, Garden City, N.Y.: Doubleday & Co., 1974, p. 437).

Scripture rather consistently mentions prophets after apostles in such passages as 1 Corinthians 12:28; Ephesians 2:20; 3:5; 4:11; and Revelation 18:20. As stated previously, prophets are given the distinguished position of foundational standing (EPH. 2:20). In fact they appear at the head of the list with the saints in a special group of those who are to be ultimately rewarded (REV. 11:18; 16:6; 18:24).

The measure of a true prophet is determined by the ultimate reality—the truth—of what he or she has spoken. The determining factor is whether what those who claim to be prophets (or are considered such) have spoken is true or becomes a reality. That, in turn, determines whether their calling is from the Spirit of God or not.

> You may say to yourself, "How can we recognize a word that the Lord has not spoken?" If a prophet speaks in the name of the Lord but the thing does not take place or prove true, it is a word that the Lord has not spoken. The prophet has spoken it presumptuously; do not be frightened by it (DEUT. 18:21-22).

Barth attempts to tie all this together by stating:

> As shown earlier, the epistle to the Ephesians especially emphasizes the close tie between Israel and the church and makes intensive use of Israel's Bible. At the same time, 2:20 may add and emphasize something else that is worthy of attention.

> It may be that only NT prophets and apostles are meant, i.e. men witnessing explicitly to Jesus Christ (*Ephesians 4–6*, Garden City, N.Y.: Doubleday & Co., 1974, p. 315).

What does all this mean for us today? What is a prophetic office? Much of the confusion arises from the fact that prophecy to most people means predicting the future. It is difficult for many people to realize that prophecy speaks not only about and for the future, but also has a specific word for the present.

The Greek noun *prophetes* is related to the verb *propheteuo*, which means "to speak forth, to say, to declare openly, to make known publicly, to proclaim," or "making public declaration." Ultimately the verb came to have the meaning of speaking of matters "in advance" or "before," that is, "to predict."

Gerhard Friedrich says:

> All prophecy rests on revelation, I C. 14:30. The prophet does not declare what he has taken from tradition or what he has thought up himself. He declares what has been revealed to him. The *apokalupsis* of I C. 14:26 is the revelation which is imparted to the prophet and which is to become prophetic

proclamation in the congregation, I C. 14:26-30. Thus
prophecy is very closely related to revelation. I C. 14:6, 30;
Eph. 3:5; I Pt. 1:10-12. God is the subject in revelation, but
only indirectly the subject in prophecy.

As I C. 14 deals with prophecy and tongues, so I C. 13:8-12
deals with prophecy and knowledge (*gnosis*). Both are
charismata, both are concerned with the knowledge of
mysteries, and both are fragmentary rather than definitive or
perfect. *Gnosis* is not set above prophecy in I C. 13:2 for
prophecy rather than *gnosis* is for Paul the supreme gift of
grace. They differ in the way that the knowledge of mysteries
is attained and in the use to which this knowledge is put.
Gnosis is one of the "rational gifts of the Spirit." In contrast,
prophecy rests on inspiration. Knowledge is given to it by
sudden revelation. The prophetic thought or image strikes the
prophet from without (*Theological Dictionary of the New
Testament*, vol. 6, Grand Rapids: Wm. B. Eerdmans, 1982, pp.
853–54).

Prophetic ministry continues among us. It is a gift bestowed on
individuals by the Spirit of God to bring a specific message to his people.
The prophet can make mistakes. A prophet is not infallible. Therefore, he or she must also have the humility to be open to correction
by the rest of the body of Christ, as C. P. Wagner states:

Those who receive the benefit of the gift of prophecy can
expect comfort, guidance, warning, encouragement,
admonition, judgment and edification. Some prophecies are
directed by God to individuals, some to the Body of Christ as
a whole. . . . Once the spiritual gift is confirmed by the Body,
the person with the gift should be highly respected, and his or
her words received with confidence (*Your Spiritual Gifts*,
Ventura, Calif.: GL Publications, 1985, p. 229).

Any Christian through whom the Lord determines by his grace to
speak a word needs to walk in humility. Any sense of pride is a hindrance
to the Spirit of God. Strong stubborn feelings that have roots in the

flesh bring problems, but "strong sensitive feelings" that trace themselves to the heart of God are indications that there is "a prophet in our midst." The sage of old said, "Where there is no vision, the people perish" (PROV. 29:18 KJV).

If we desire to follow reliable guidance that enables us to be fruitful and productive in the kingdom of God, we need to be alert to the prophets that God raises to the surface in the church. They are the individuals that add a new dimension of vision to the life of the church.

The prophetic office in this Ephesians text, however, is one that is an official capacity. This office gift might be manifested in a local congregation or the church at large, wherever an individual is recognized as having a prophetic gift. These are individuals with a gift of vision. They see things in the present and in the future that others may readily overlook. When recognized in an official manner, they can provide direction to the body of Christ. Nevertheless, because all of us are yet sinners, including prophets, we need checks and balances. The prophets need to be mature enough to have their prophetic utterances weighed so as to determine whether they are in harmony with the Word of God. The ultimate check is always whether their words do not conflict with what is already revealed in God's Word. It is as Paul states, "And the spirits of prophets are subject to the prophets, for God is a God not of disorder but of peace" (1 COR. 14:32-33).

Evangelist

The Greek word for evangelist (EPH. 4:11) is a compound of two words. The first Greek word means "well, good, kind, right, and proper," *eu*. The second word means "messenger, envoy, one sent, an angel of God," *aggelos*. Evangelist conveys one who is a good messenger, a messenger who comes to bring good news—news that will fill a listener's heart with joy and thanksgiving.

In biblical times most messages were brought by messengers who came on foot. Messengers would be the bearers of either good news or bad news. Good news, of course, was always more welcome. Eventually, the name given to a messenger of good news was "evangelist." Applied to the message of the gospel, evangelism implied the special function of announcing to sinners the special blessing of forgiveness of sins through the atonement of Jesus Christ on the cross for their sins. It was a delightful and welcome announcement of good news that a person could get right with God through Christ. The individual who brought such news was known as an evangelist—a bearer of good news.

Such individuals were not specifically called to serve a specific congregation but moved about from place to place, proclaiming the gospel to people wherever they had an opportunity. In this respect, evangelism took on an even broader meaning.

Who then is an evangelist? How do we know or recognize such an individual? How do we identify this gift? An evangelistic gift can be recognized in a person who has an insatiable desire to share the love of God in Christ with people. This can manifest itself in either one-on-one situations, or in a broader perspective with larger groups of people. Some have made a distinction between the personal evangelist and the public evangelist. But both have one dynamic in common: their motivation to share the love of God in Christ.

Evangelists share the gospel of Jesus Christ in such a manner that it becomes good news to the hearers. The hearers respond and become faithful and committed followers of Jesus Christ. The evangelist also has a specific anointing "to equip the saints, for the work of ministry, for building up the body of Christ" (EPH. 4:12). The official recognition of such individuals within the congregation and in the church at large enables the process of bringing people to faith in Christ. When evangelists are able to act freely, they can function so much more effectively in sharing the message from God that is in their hearts. The office of evangelist has been recognized in the church in the past and this recognition has brought forth fruit in many ways.

Pastor

In order to understand the term *pastor* (EPH. 4:11) more fully, we need to understand the frequent use of metaphors in the Bible. Metaphors are figures of speech that utilize one kind of expression or thing in place of another, suggesting a likeness between them. If the analogy is not understood properly, the point is lost or may be entirely misunderstood.

This is important to remember in order to understand the word *pastor*. The term comes from the Latin and can be translated as "shepherd" or "sheep-herder." (The Greek term used in Ephesians 4:11 for pastor is *poimen*.) This does not mean that a pastor is literally a person who has a ranch with sheep. Rather it is an analogy that suggests similarities which, if understood, will add much insight to understanding the ministry of the pastor.

Who and what is a pastor? Alexander Cruden tells us,

> The original meaning of this word was shepherd, and in this sense it is sometimes used in the Bible. The Eastern shepherd must both protect and feed his sheep—so there is derived the meaning of spiritual leader, minister, one given charge of a church of Christ, to care for spiritual interests of the people and feed their souls with spiritual food. This meaning is also found in the Bible (*Cruden's Complete Concordance*, Grand Rapids: Zondervan, 1949, p. 483).

The specific characteristic of this ministry can best be determined by studying the characteristics of a good shepherd. A shepherd was one who loved his sheep. Jesus is the ultimate shepherd. Jesus said,

> I am the good shepherd (*poimen*). The good shepherd lays down his life for the sheep. I lay down my life for the sheep. And I have other sheep, that are not of this fold; I must bring them also, and they will heed my voice (JOHN 10:11).

Pastors are shepherds of their flocks. They have a love and concern for those to whom they are called. They have a concern for the lost, the sick, the maimed, the lonely. They have as loving a concern for the sheep as for their own well-being.

One of the specific characteristics of a shepherd is that the shepherd is always at the head of the flock, never behind the flock to push or drive them forward but at the head leading them on the proper path to their destination. The shepherd does not yell and shout, but speaks specific commands with vested authority and the sheep respond.

The sheep respond because they have come to trust in the shepherd who has clearly demonstrated great love for them—love that is without a selfish motive.

What then is the pastoral ministry or office? C. P. Wagner describes this office gift:

> The gift of pastor is the special ability that God gives to certain members of the Body of Christ to assume a long-term

personal responsibility for the spiritual welfare of a group of believers.

The word "pastor" itself is borrowed from animal husbandry, particularly sheep raising. It is by no means as universally an understood vocation today as it was in the first century Palestine, so it needs some explanation. The pastor of a group of Christians is the person responsible under Jesus, who is the Master Shepherd, for teaching, feeding, healing the wounds, developing unity, helping people find their gifts, and doing whatever else is necessary to see that they continue in faith and grow in their spiritual lives.

Several biblical words are used as synonyms for pastor. The English words elder, presbyter, overseer, and bishop (sometimes interchanged depending on the translation) all mean pastor. Because these words are used in such a variety of ways in our contemporary churches, it is helpful to distinguish between the office of pastor and the gift of pastor. Most of those we call pastors in America are people occupying the office of pastor. They have a staff position in the church. The point I am making here is that not everyone who has the office of pastor needs the gift of pastor, and furthermore there are many men and women with the gift of pastor who do not have the office of pastor by being placed on a church staff (*Your Spiritual Gifts*, Ventura, Calif.: GL Publications, 1985, p. 143).

As we study the other categories of gifts, we will discover why there may be differences in how one pastor ministers as compared with another. Such differences are related to the other categorical gifts the pastors have been given. This will become clearer as we review the various personality gifts.

What then is the specific responsibility of a pastor? First, the pastor is under the headship of Christ who is the head of the church. Pastors receive their directions from Christ, the head shepherd.

Also, the pastor of a group of Christians is the person responsible for equipping the saints to minister, for teaching, counseling, healing, bringing harmony and more. The pastor instructs people to enable them to discover their gifts and to minister to the needs of those around them. These people in turn lead more people to the assurance of their salvation in Christ and equip them for ministry to the body of Christ. In these ways, the pastor demonstrates to the sheep the way to be empowered by the Holy Spirit so they can be productive, fruitful servants of the Lord.

Teacher

The last office gift listed in Ephesians 4:11 is that of teacher. This gift presents a problem. All the other gifts in this account are preceded with the article *tous* (translated as "some"), but the gift "teacher" has no article. Is something implied in this little omission, or are we making something out of nothing?

Various scholars present a good argument for the interpretation of a combination pastor-teacher association. These scholars believe that these are not two gifts but one in combination. Their reasoning is that a pastor has to be "an apt teacher" (1 TIM. 3:2). It is interesting that this Ephesians account is the only account that mentions pastor, and the term is here closely associated with teacher.

It is logical to presume that there can be very little pastoral care without teaching, either directly or indirectly. In this respect this gift would be different from the gift mentioned in Romans 12:6-8. Perhaps we can best define it as a pastoral teaching gift. It is a teaching gift closely aligned with the pastoral responsibility of equipping the saints so they are able to discover who they are in the kingdom and effectively build up the body of Christ.

QUESTIONS FOR DISCUSSION OR REFLECTION

1. Do you believe that the term *apostle* should only be applied to the twelve New Testament apostles, or that the gift of apostolic ministry continues even in our day?

2. Why did Paul emphasize the gift of prophecy so much? Is prophecy necessary for the church today? Why or why not? What scriptural basis is there for your answer?

3. How can we recognize that someone has the gift of an evangelist? What are the characteristics of such a person?

CHAPTER 4

Personality Gifts

ROMANS 12:1-8

In order to understand properly Paul's intent in Romans 12:1-8, to which we now turn, we need to understand the factors that led to the composition of the letter to the Romans. The writer's basic objectives play a leading role in proper interpretation of the meaning of any biblical passage, including this one.

For several years the apostle Paul had had a keen desire to go to Rome in order to proclaim the message of salvation through Christ (ROM. 1:13; 15:22). When he was in Ephesus he stated, "I must also see Rome" (ACTS 19:21).

It seems quite likely that Paul wrote the letter between A.D. 54–58 while he was in the house of Gaius in Corinth (ROM. 16:23; 1 COR. 1:14). He longed to share the gospel with all so they could come to the assurance of salvation (ROM. 1:13) even as he had come to such assurance. Moreover, he desired that they would become productive disciples in the kingdom of God.

This letter is different from the letters to the Ephesians and Corinthians in that Paul does not specifically seek to deal with false doctrines or warn against specific weaknesses that might endanger the life of the congregation. Rather, he simply wishes to proclaim to these people a gospel that is free of law. In this letter he presents the gospel in a quiet, systematic, and orderly manner.

For almost all of the first three chapters he demonstrates that without Christ people are under the wrath and condemnation of God. But Christ has atoned for our sins and obtained the righteousness of God for us through his death on the cross (ROM. 3:21-26). This righteousness of God is available to all by faith in Christ. Paul then proceeds to demonstrate the secure, fruitful life of one who is endowed with the Spirit of Christ:

> But you are not in the flesh, you are in the Spirit, since the Spirit of God dwells in you. Anyone who does not have the Spirit of Christ does not belong to him (ROM. 8:9).

This subsequently leads to the introduction of the specific category of gifts that will be referred to as personality gifts. Paul introduces them somewhat casually when he says,

> I beseech, I appeal to you brothers, by the mercies of God, to present, consecrate, dedicate your bodies (*somata*), your individuality, your personality, as a living offering—a sacrifice (ROM. 12:1 paraphrased).

A much more understandable term for *soma* today is "personality." Personality in today's understanding implies the personal identity, existence, and quality of the entire person. As previously stated, this translation has limitations. The word *soma* means something more than body and personality. It basically means all of a person and not just one's physical being. Paul had in mind the entire person: body, soul, and spirit.

The charismata listed in Romans 12 could be called "diaconal gifts," gifts to be used in ministry and service. Yet there are limitations to such a description since one of the specific gifts mentioned in 12:7 (*diakonia*, ministry in RSV) is a "diaconal gift" in the literal sense of the term. More is intended by Paul's terminology than our present English is able to put into one word.

Paul continues by calling on his readers to present their entire being, entire personality, entire person to the Lord so that the Lord might do a work in each individual person. These words give the impression that the gifts he lists are latent or dormant in an individual. However, when the individual personality is presented to the Lord, the Spirit of God endows that individual with power so the specific dormant gifts come to fruition. This latency might be compared to salvation which is available to every individual, but is dormant until the atonement of

Christ is appropriated in that person by the power of the Holy Spirit. The Gospel of John speaks specifically to that subject:

> But the Advocate, the Holy Spirit, whom the Father will send in my name, will teach you everything, and remind you of all that I have said to you (JOHN 14:26).

> When the Advocate comes, whom I will send to you from the Father, the Spirit of truth who comes from the Father, he will testify on my behalf. You also are to testify because you have been with me from the beginning (JOHN 15:26-27).

> When the Spirit of truth comes, he will guide you into all the truth; for he will not speak on his own, but will speak whatever he hears, and he will declare to you the things that are to come (JOHN 16:13).

> Until now you have not asked for anything in my name. Ask and you will receive, so that your joy may be complete (JOHN 16:24).

Referring to the group of gifts in Romans 12:6-8 as personality gifts may limit them to some extent, but this terminology provides more of what Paul intended than the word *soma* (body) or diaconal gifts. After his appeal in 12:1, Paul exhorts,

> And be not fashioned, conformed, or assimilated to the world; but be transformed, reshaped, and changed (*metamorphousthe*) with the renewing of the mind (ROM. 12:2 paraphrased).

After this introduction, Paul begins to expound on these gifts that are associated or peculiar to the personality of the individual. Paul does not state that they are "all in all" (*ta panta en pasin*). Rather, the emphasis is on a variation of gifts that will likely differ from one individual to another. Paul begins with an emphasis on having gifts that differ (*diaphora*), after which he goes on to list the various personality gifts: prophecy, ministry (service), teaching, exhortation, giving, leading (administration), and compassion (mercy).

Paul sees specific, unique characteristics in individual personalities. A person may have one or more of these specific personality gifts, but each has at least one which makes him or her unique. As individuals become aware of their specific personality gifts, they are enabled to know how they fit into the body of Christ and how they can make a positive contribution to that body with a measure of confidence. The question may be asked, "Cannot these traits also be learned rather than be innate qualities?" It may be possible that some of the qualities may be learned, but for those who are endowed with a specific personality gift, developing it fully is much easier and takes less effort.

An individual who is endowed with a mercy gift is naturally attracted to and has a great deal of compassion for the poor or disabled. The person with a teaching personality has a natural ability to teach. Another person without such a gift of teaching may also teach, but with much more effort.

The above description does not mean that only the individuals with a teaching personality are to teach; rather it helps explain why some individuals find it much easier to teach than others. Knowing this will also cause less confusion, jealousy, and insecurity. The result is much greater unity, harmony, and joy in the body of Christ, for all can see that they are endowed with a specific unique personality gift or gifts that can be employed to bring a valuable blessing to the entire body of believers.

However, a danger needs to be considered. Sometimes others find it relatively easy to take advantage of individuals with a specific personality gift. Individuals with specific gifts need to be protected. The people who are most able to show mercy will quickly burn out if they are asked to carry the burdens of everyone around them. The servers will also be overwhelmed if they are called to serve in every specific circumstance.

In this respect we need to take a closer look at each of the personality gifts to discern the specific characteristics that may enable individuals to identify the gifts.

Prophecy

The first of the gifts listed in Romans 12:6-8 is prophecy. The word *prophecy* is another of those terms that comes from a combination of Greek words. We have already made reference to this under the office gifts. The first word is *pro* meaning "for," "before," "in front of," and "at." The second part of the word is *phemi*, meaning "to see to it," "to say," "to affirm," "to tell." Putting the two words together we see that prophecy means to foretell. Some have narrowly interpreted this to mean that prophets are able to predict the future. This interpretation leaves out any application for the present.

The basic meaning of prophecy is to have a specific word for a specific situation and to proclaim it. God gives the gift of prophecy to people to enable them to proclaim a message directed toward a person, church, situation, or circumstance. A key difference between the prophetic ministry mentioned in Ephesians 4:11 and the prophetic personality gift is that prophetic ministry is a vocation—a call from the Holy Spirit. The personality gift of prophecy is an expression that functions more individually and perhaps occasionally, whereas the prophetic ministry functions more in an official capacity over the entire body for a longer period of time.

Since "all have sinned and fall short" (ROM. 3:23), prophets make mistakes. Therefore, they must also be open to correction by the rest of the body of believers. As with all other things in life, prophecy needs to be evaluated and mistakes corrected. Those with prophetic person-alities need to have the maturity to be corrected when there is reason to believe that mistakes have been made in their proclamation of a prophetic message.

Also, others like Luther have associated prophecy with preaching. There may be prophecy in preaching, that is, some prophecy may manifest itself through preaching, but preaching of itself is not nec-essarily prophetic.

Another aspect of prophecy is social consciousness. Prophets were among the most socially conscious of all the people described in God's Word. They often spoke out with a word from the heart of God against injustice and indifference to public righteousness, not from their own astuteness but because they were attuned to the heart of God.

Prophets are quick to see injustice and ungodliness. They are bur-dened by the destruction and lawlessness they see and forcibly speak out against it. Prophets often say what needs to be said, but individuals or society in general do not desire to hear it. The result is that prophets readily become fatalities. In Scripture we read that prophets often died a martyr's death. People do not desire to hear the truth as revealed from the lips of a prophet.

Ministry (Service)

The second gift listed in Romans 12:6-8 is *diakonia*. This word has frequently been translated as "ministry," which is correct. However, the word *ministry* has come to have a rather limited meaning in light of its contemporary understanding in America. Another broader word to translate this specific personality gift is "service." This gift is more task oriented.

An individual with this specific gift is the first to volunteer for specific tasks when volunteers are requested. Servers may leave other responsibilities to serve others. This more than likely gets them into trouble with their own families who may feel neglected.

They do not serve to gain attention or recognition. They simply have within them a specific need or calling to serve. They are individuals who, when they see a task that needs doing, do it and do it without fanfare or recognition. It is relatively easy for a body of believers to take advantage of such servers, allowing them to do all the menial tasks and thereby drive them to exhaustion. Therefore, it also becomes important to protect individuals with specific gifts so that others do not take advantage of them.

The Greek word for server is *diakonos* and is often translated "deacon" or "deaconess." In the New Testament the term *deacon* or *deaconess* was used in connection with "waiting on tables" (LUKE 17:8; 12:37; 22:26), supervising a meal (ACTS 6:2, LUKE 10:40, JOHN 12:2), or serving others by supplying food, shelter, and clothes. Servers also feel drawn to help the sick and imprisoned. Herman W. Beyer elaborates on this gift by saying,

> Jesus' view of service grows out of the OT command of love for one's neighbor, which He takes and links with the command of love for God to constitute the substance of the divinely willed ethical conduct of His followers. In so doing, He purifies the concept of service from the distortions which it had suffered in Judaism. Jesus' attitude to service is completely new as compared with the Greek understanding. The decisive point is that He sees in it the thing which makes man His disciple (*Theological Dictionary of the New Testament*, vol. 2, Grand Rapids: Wm. B. Eerdmans, 1982, p. 135).

Teaching

The Greek word for teaching (*didasko*) is a relatively common word. It is defined with such words as "teach," "learn," and "instruct." It has reference to both teaching and learning. Friedrich Buchsel states,

> The word calls attention to two aspects, being applied on one side to the insight of the one who is to be instructed and on the other to the knowledge presupposed in the teacher. In relation to the second aspect, especially when it is a question of practical arts and crafts, the example of the teacher forms a bridge to the knowledge and ability of the pupil (*Theological Dictionary of the New Testament*, vol. 2, Grand Rapids: Wm. B. Eerdmans, 1982, p. 135).

Teaching is also a basic general responsibility of every Christian as Jesus commanded when he said, "Make disciples . . . baptizing . . . teaching them to obey everything that I have commanded you" (MATT. 28:19-20). All Christians need to teach the Word of God, whether they are endowed with this personality gift or not.

Teaching personalities find special delight in studying the Word of God to discover and confirm divine truth. At times it may seem they find as much joy in studying God's Word, or whatever subject they are considering, as they do in presenting what they have discovered.

Christians who have a teaching personality have a great deal of respect for the authority of the Bible. They are inclined to place a great deal of emphasis on accuracy and will often quote their sources word for word. They are also inclined to check any quotations and comments they discover in other authors for accuracy and context. They want to make sure that what is said is not simply stated to make a specific point but also correctly quoted and interpreted.

Christian teachers also have a tendency to stick rather closely to the subject, especially Scripture. They do not want nonscriptural information to detract from God's Word. This does not mean that they do not use nonbiblical material to illustrate, but that they are cautious in what they use. Even those with this personality gift who teach in a secular field have a tendency, either directly or indirectly, to find ways to share biblical insights, passages, or incidents.

I am reminded of an individual with a Jewish heritage but who was of no particular faith. In a secular classroom he consistently quoted various portions of Scripture to illustrate points in the psychology and philosophy courses he was teaching. It seemed natural for him to come back to the Word of God. In addition, it seemed he had a hunger to search out the truth.

Teaching personalities are also quick to discern when a passage or portion of Scripture is taken out of context. As a result, they will devote a great deal of time to determine the specific context of a certain subject or text that is studied.

Teaching personalities will consistently seek guidance directly from the Spirit of God, even though they realize the valuable assistance they can get from commentaries and other resources. But they tend to test and prove the teachings received from such books or from other people to make sure they are in harmony with God's Word.

Teachers have the unique ability to make deep, profound concepts simple and understandable in much the same way that Jesus did. They present the Word of God in an orderly and systematic manner. Teachers sometimes err in wanting to present too much detail and thus their classes become boring and irrelevant to the learners. A teaching personality may also have a weakness to become content- rather than learner-oriented. Sometimes teachers may quit being learners themselves and become irrelevant with outdated teaching. This is unfortunate because the Word of God is always relevant.

Exhortation

Exhortation (ROM. 12:8) is a personality gift that is frequently misunderstood. It is often misinterpreted and given a negative connotation. We are able to get a much better understanding of this gift as we study the definition in its original language.

The Greek word for exhortation is *parakaleo*, which has a wide variety of meanings. It means "to summon, call upon for help, appeal to, urge, encourage, comfort, implore, cheer up." One of the names for the Holy Spirit, Paraclete, comes from this same root and is translated the "comforter" or the "advocate."

People with this gift have the motivation to bring comfort and encouragement to someone who needs them. It is a gift that brings out the best in others. It is a personality gift that encourages people when they really need a word of encouragement.

The exhorter has been called the cheerleader or coach in the church. When the exhorters see people struggling and ready to give up, they come with a word of encouragement that enables such people to continue striving until they have reached their maximum potential.

This gift is different from prophecy in that prophecy at times can have a rather negative emphasis, whereas this gift is more positive. The exhorter is one who desires to see the Word become a reality in the members of the body of Christ. So the exhorter is one who consistently urges people onward in their walk with God.

Exhorters are able to lay out specific goals for people and provide practical steps for action. They may provide words of wisdom and knowledge that are also words of comfort and encouragement.

An example of this gift in Scripture may well be Paul's coworker, Barnabas, who was also referred to as "son of encouragement" (ACTS 4:36). It was Barnabas who stood by Paul when others questioned the validity of his apostleship and conversion experience with the Lord. It was Barnabas who recognized the potential in John Mark when Paul for some unknown reason did not wish to take Mark with them (COL. 4:10; ACTS 15:36-41).

All Christians are called to be a source of comfort to each other, "encouraging one another, and all the more as you see the Day approaching" (HEB. 10:25). But some Christians have been endowed with this special gift of exhortation by which they are able to bring out the best in others. That is not only a blessing to them but to others as well. It is to our advantage to help these people to discover their gift, so that they in turn may also help others to discover all their gifts and abilities.

Giving

If we do not properly understand the personality gifts, we will certainly have trouble understanding the gift of giving (ROM. 12:8). All Christians are called to give. Scripture admonishes us, "Give, and it shall be given to you" (LUKE 6:38). Every Christian should set specific goals and give joyfully. This is a Christian responsibility, and there are no exceptions. The rich and the poor, children and parents, young and old: all are called to give. The admonitions are quite clear, "God is not mocked; for you reap whatever you sow" (GAL. 6:7).

Giving and generosity are synonymous with everything the Christian faith stands for. However, this personality gift implies something additional that is not necessarily true of all Christians. The personality gift of giving has specific characteristics that identify it.

Some individuals are endowed with a specific gift of generosity. It does not take long to recognize such people. They are quick to share their home, time, and possessions. It seems that the Lord blesses them for their generosity. It may well be that because of their generosity the Lord is able to bless them, for the more they have, the more they give.

People with the gift of giving or generosity have a sensitivity for the needs of others. They not only sense the needs but also are quick to respond even before there is an appeal. They give willingly, generously, and often anonymously. They prefer to give in a manner so that their left hand does not know what the right hand does (MATT. 6:3-4).

These individuals often live more simply than they are capable of living, enabling them to have more to give away. Frequently they will gather a fairly large sum of money in anticipation of a great need that may arise in the future and at the right moment give either the entire amount or a large sum to that specific need. Givers invariably are faithful tithers but also give offerings far beyond their tithe.

Abraham is a good example of one who had this gift of giving. We are informed that he was "very rich in livestock, in silver, and in gold" (GEN. 13:2). Yet he dealt charitably with Lot his nephew, giving him the richest lands while he was content with what Lot did not want.

Givers are easy targets for the greedy. They are also easy targets for other Christians who approach them with specific projects and appeals. Frequently, givers who are so sensitive to need will respond to such appeals, but are sometimes deeply hurt when they discover that someone has taken advantage of their gift of generosity. They need to ask God's guidance so that they are wise in the use of this good gift.

Leading (Administration)

The word that is translated "leadership" or "administration" in Romans 12:8 is a fascinating word and has been translated in various ways. The word literally means "one who stands in front of." The Greek word traces itself to the word *proistemi*, which comes from two Greek words.

The first word is *pro*, which means "before," "in front of." The second word is *istemi*, which means "to make to stand," "set," "place," "appoint," or "establish." Together they mean "to put before, to place over, to stand in front of, to appoint with authority." In other words, the term means "to put in place of leadership."

> In most instances *proistemi* seems to have sense a. "to lead" but the context shows in each case that one must also take into account sense b. "to care for." This is explained by the fact that caring was the obligation of leading members of the infant church. . . . Thus Paul says in Romans 12:28 . . . The meaning, then, is somewhat as follows: "He who gives let him do so with simplicity, he who *cares* with zeal, he who does good with cheerfulness" (*Theological Dictionary of the New Testament*, vol. 6, Grand Rapids: Wm. B. Eerdmans, 1982, p. 701).

These individuals have the ability to organize people and circumstances so all can function to their best ability in the caring of the entire body of Christ. They have organizational and leadership ability to enable the body of Christ to fulfill its ministry. It does not take long to recognize these individuals. They invariably carry a little book that outlines and details the activities of the week or day. They have the ability to see quickly the overall picture. Once they have established the overall picture they once again are quick to help the group establish goals and guidelines to reach them.

Those with the gift of leadership not only are capable of organizing but also are able of delegating responsibilities and motivating people to participate. They do this by giving clear descriptions as to what and how the task is to be done and why it is important. After that they follow up on the instructions to determine whether the work is being carried out the way the group intended. If not, they are likely to insist on it being done properly and expeditiously.

Leaders are frequently subject to criticism because they find themselves in key positions of leadership. But criticism does not often stop them from fulfilling their objectives. They are capable of remaining strong in the midst of negative reactions. They are willing to listen to anything that will enable the group's specific objectives to be accomplished since they long to get the work done quickly and efficiently.

Leaders derive a great deal of joy in seeing accomplished projects. They will often work long, feverish hours, and until the project that they are responsible for is completed there is no time for them to relax. Once it is finished, the leaders may become restless and uneasy. They long for another challenge to occupy their time and ability. Leaders have a natural tendency to take on responsibility. When a specific task needs to be organized and done in a specific setting, they are likely to assume the responsibility if no other leadership surfaces to get it accomplished. On the other hand, if other leadership emerges, they may stay in the background until they are asked to lead. They may also be the most vocal critics of poor leadership.

Nehemiah in the Old Testament is a good example of one who had such leadership ability. He was able to gather the people together and in the midst of all kinds of threats was able to organize the people and rebuild the temple.

Compassion (Mercy)

Similar to exhortation and prophecy, the gift of compassion or mercy (ROM. 12:8) is highly intuitive and sensitive. It might be called the gift of empathy. It is more than sympathy. A person endowed with this gift is able to discern hurts and heartaches in others that may not be readily apparent to most people. These individuals are not afraid to engage in one-on-one relationships with individuals who are suffering physically, emotionally, or spiritually. They are more inclined to emphasize gospel than law. Their basic desire is to bring a word of encouragement to the discouraged, a word of hope to the hopeless, some light to the darkness.

Among the beneficiaries of the gift of compassion and mercy are the ill, the grieving, the homeless, the retarded, the prisoners, the blind, the poor, the abused, the shut-in. The compassionate person cannot easily pass by the needy, wherever they might be.

While every Christian is called to show mercy, those with this gift have a tendency to demonstrate compassion and mercy as a part of their life-style. They continually seek opportunities to show pity to the suffering. They are the Mother Teresas of the world.

Dorcas is a good biblical example of the gift of mercy. Scripture informs us that her life was an example of deeds of kindness and compassion. She was one who empathized with the widows and orphans.

She made garments for the poor and distributed them to those who needed them (ACTS 9:36ff).

Another example of this gift is the good Samaritan. The religious leaders could pass by the wounded man on the side of the road, but the good Samaritan had to stop. He not only stopped to help but also bound the man's wounds and made sure he was being taken care of before he continued on (LUKE 10:30-37).

Personality Gifts Encouraged and Protected

Individuals with various gifts need to be encouraged in their gifts. It is fitting for the body of Christ to make its members aware of what their specific gift or gifts might be. People need that kind of affirmation. It is often hard for people to discern their gift or gifts. Some think it is arrogant or an indication of false pride to state what they believe to be their gifts. Therefore, they are tremendously encouraged when others confirm what those people's specific personality gifts might be.

In the same respect members of the body of Christ also need to shield and sustain each other so some do not become overburdened. It is easy for individuals both in and out of the church to take advantage of the givers, the leaders, the compassionate, the servers, the teachers, and all who have the various personality gifts. In taking advantage of such people, we ultimately discourage or destroy them and as a result we are all the poorer. For instance, compassionate people are not able to take care of all the hurting. They need to be sustained and preserved from becoming overburdened. The givers need to be protected from the constant appeals from others. The leaders need to be protected from too much responsibility in too many areas. The servers need to be protected from being called to serve everywhere and everyone while their own loved ones are neglected. Each specific personality gift needs to be affirmed but also shielded for the benefit of all in the body of Christ.

QUESTIONS FOR DISCUSSION OR REFLECTION

1. Why would someone with a prophetic personality see injustice and ungodliness sooner than many other people?

2. When individuals have been endowed with the gift of ministry, how do they need to be protected so their lives remain balanced?

3. What are some of the joys that will be experienced by a person with a teaching gift, or a gift of exhortation, or giving, or mercy? Where do you see your gifts?

4. What people have you known who are blessed with the ability to organize or lead? In what ways is it a blessing to be working in a group that has a capable leader?

CHAPTER 5

Manifestational Gifts

1 CORINTHIANS 12:4-11

The last group of charismata we will consider are listed in 1 Corinthians 12:4-11. We refer to them as "manifestational gifts" because that is how Paul introduces them when he writes, "To each is given the manifestation of the Spirit for the common good" (12:7).

It is quite likely that Paul wrote this letter on his third missionary journey while he was in Ephesus around A.D. 53–57 (1 COR. 16:8; ACTS 19:1-41). He had learned that things were not at all well in the Corinthian church. He had been there earlier and had taken up residence with friends, Aquila and Priscilla (ACTS 18:1-3). He had preached in the synagogue with great success. With support from Timothy and Silas from Macedonia he had put forth additional effort and argued persuasively about the kingdom of God, but the people were so obstinate that he was forced to leave the synagogue.

His most notable convert was a man named Crispus who was the ruler of the synagogue in Corinth (ACTS 18:8). The Jews resisted to the point of bringing Paul before Gallio, the Roman governor, on a charge of teaching things contrary to the law. But Gallio, with impartial justice, refused to hear them. It was a time of suspicion and tension.

Shortly afterwards, a delegation of leaders from the church in Corinth arrived in Ephesus where Paul was preaching to consult with him about some serious problems and disorders that had arisen among the Christians in Corinth. It was probably during this time that Paul wrote the first letter to the Corinthians. One question that Paul was asked to deal with was the matter of spiritual gifts, specifically the charismata that are referred to in chapter 12 of this letter.

Apparently pride and arrogance had caused a great deal of dissension among the believers. So Paul begins by saying, "Now concerning spiritual gifts" (1 COR. 12:1). The word in Greek is *pneumatikon*, a genitive plural that could be translated literally with the word *spirituals*. The apparent reference is to the people who were endowed with the Spirit of God. Somehow in expression of that endowment, they were causing confusion and dissension among the believers.

Immediately Paul begins to deal with this problem. In verse 4, he clarifies and broadens his interpretation by stating, "Now there are varieties (*diaireseis*) of gifts (*charismaton*)." He proceeds to clarify to whom these gifts (*charismata*) are given or distributed in verse 6 when he states, "But it is the same God who activates (*energon*) all (*panta*) of them in everyone" (*en pasin*). This immediately gives us a different perspective from the gifts mentioned in Ephesians 4:11-12, where the emphasis is on "some" (*men-de*).

The language used points to a particular calling for some to the exclusion of others. The same is true in Romans 12:6-8, where the emphasis is on having "gifts that differ" (*diaphora*). In Romans, the emphasis is on the different personality gifts that enable people to bring blessings to the body of Christ through that variety. However, in the 1 Corinthians text we find a completely different emphasis stated at the very beginning (v. 6) in the words, "God who activates all of them in everyone" (*ta panta en pasin*).

Paul is apparently saying that these gifts are for everyone. This is clarified even more when in vs. 7 he states that the (*phanerosis*) manifestation, evidencing, clear display, shining (*ekasto*) is given to each, everyone, individually, for all to benefit, for the common good (paraphrased). This states that the charismata mentioned here are for the general and beneficial use of all. No one in the body of Christ is to be excluded. But neither is anyone to feel proud and utilize them proudly or selfishly, for they are available to all for the benefit of all.

After having enumerated all the gifts in vss. 8-10, Paul clarifies the utilization of those gifts and states that the Spirit dispenses and controls the energizing of those gifts. (*Panta*) all are (*energei*) activated, empowered, energized, put into operation by the one and the same Spirit, dividing or allotting (*ekasto*) to each, (*elasto*) one, all, (*idia*) individually, specially assigned (*kathos*) just as, according as, in proportion as in what manner, at what moment, when (*bouletai*) he wills, desires, chooses, pleases, wishes.

Paul states that these gifts are for all believers. They are given to all for the benefit of all. However, the Spirit dispenses them. Furthermore, the Spirit decides where, when, and at what moment to dispense the gifts. It would, therefore, seem out of order for an individual to proclaim as an example, "I always have the gift of wisdom" or "I always have the gift of healing." Rather, the appropriate interpretation would be: at the appropriate moment, when there is a specific need for ministry— when there is a need for faith, for wisdom, for knowledge, or healing— at that specific moment the Spirit activates the gifts as or when the Holy Spirit chooses.

These gifts are for everyone. The emphasis in vs. 7 and vs. 11 is on (ekasto) "each," (panto) "all," and (idia) "individually." Frederick Bruner puts it well when he says,

> And "all these [gifts] are inspired by one and the same Spirit, who apportions to each individually as he wills" (v. 11). Spiritual gifts (or to use Paul's expression, graces) are not confined to a select few who, perhaps, can exhibit extraordinary manifestations as a result of their deeper dedication or greater nearness to the Spirit. The whole variety of gifts—from the more sober to the more ecstatic—"all" are being continually apportioned (present tense verb) by the one Spirit to *each* person as the *spirit* wills. The Spirit's "gifting" work in the church is both completely universal and completely individual: he gives of all to each (A *Theology of the Holy Spirit*, Grand Rapids: Wm. B. Eerdmans, 1982, p. 290).

We can therefore conclude that these charismata are available to those with specific office gifts. These charismata are meant to empower people with office gifts in order to function more effectively "to equip the saints for the work of ministry, for building up the body of Christ."

The charismata described in 1 Corinthians are also available to all with specific personality gifts. These manifestational gifts are meant to enable those with the personality gifts to function effectively for the benefit of the entire body.

These gifts are for all to the benefit of all. They are meant to enable the believers to be more effective in witness and ministry. These manifestational gifts can be categorized in various ways. Here they will be categorized in the following manner: gifts of deeper insights, signs-and-wonders gifts, and word gifts.

Gifts of Deeper Insights

The gifts of wisdom, knowledge, and discerning of spirits belong together. The first gift in this category is introduced as "the utterance of wisdom" and "the utterance of knowledge." The words in English seem almost synonymous. However, in the Greek language both have distinct meanings. If we do not differentiate between the two we will likely end up with confusion and miss the blessing. Scripture has these insights:

> The fear of the Lord is the beginning of wisdom, and the knowledge of the Holy One is insight (PROV. 9:10).

> The fear of the Lord is the beginning of wisdom; all those who practice it have a good understanding (PS. 111:10).

Most definitions we find in commentaries are very general and do not add much clarity, as William Barclay shows when he defines wisdom as knowledge:

> The Greek word which we have translated wisdom is *sophia*. It is defined by Clement of Alexandria as "the knowledge of things human and divine and of their causes." Aristotle described it as "striving after the best ends and using the best means" (*The Letter to the Corinthians*, Philadelphia: Westminster Press, 1956, p. 121).

Although wisdom is listed first and knowledge second, we will take them in reverse order because doing so will enhance understanding the unique characteristics of each. A word of knowledge is a proclamation of truth as from the heart of God, a word from God.

A word of knowledge might best be explained as proclaiming an understanding of a truth of God or shedding light on a mystery of God. Knowledge is more than a revelation of facts that people could have come to know in another way. It is also more than mere knowing about the things of God; it is knowing the truth. We might compare knowledge to the teaching of Jesus about the relationship between Father and the Son (LUKE 10:22) and the teaching of Paul in the first part of Ephesians as it relates the plan of God.

Paul seems to allude to the difference between knowledge and wisdom when he says,

> Yet among the mature we do speak wisdom, though it is not a wisdom of this age or of the rulers of this age, who are doomed to perish. But we speak God's wisdom, secret and hidden, which God decreed before the ages for our glory. None of the rulers of this age understood this; for if they had, they would not have crucified the Lord of glory (1 COR. 2:6-8).

A word of wisdom or the utterance of wisdom adds depth and practicality to a word of knowledge. An utterance of wisdom is concerned with the best and most beneficial and practical way to live. A word of knowledge without practical application only leads to confusion, frustration, and despair because it lacks relevance.

Wisdom puts the needed relevance into knowledge and shows its practical application so that beneficial results are achieved in everyday life.

The original text in 1 Corinthians 12:28 uses both "utterance of knowledge" (*logos gnosis*) and "utterance of wisdom" (*logos sophia*). A word of knowledge has to do with the revelation and expression of truth.

Rudolf Bultmann states,

> The Old Testament view is that knowledge is insight into the will of God in command and blessing. . . . The Christian view of knowledge is thus largely determined by the Old Testament. An obedient and grateful acknowledgment of the deeds and demands of God is linked with knowledge of God and what He has done and demands (*Theological Dictionary of the New Testament*, vol. 1, Grand Rapids: Wm. B. Eerdmans, 1964, p. 707).

But wisdom gives us the practical guidance to know how to use a word of knowledge in life-enhancing ways. Gerhard Friedrich says that wisdom is

the gift of knowing God's statutes—a gift sought from God as
Ruler of the world. God dwells within us in His Word of faith,
in calling to His promise, in the wisdom of the statutes and in
the commandments of doctrine. . . . is also the divinely
revealed knowledge of the hidden secrets of God which no one
knows but the wise and understanding man and the man who
loves the Lord. . . . This wisdom is often sharply differentiated
from general human wisdom (*Theological Dictionary of the New
Testament*, vol. 7, Grand Rapids: Wm. B. Eerdmans, 1971, p.
526).

A word of knowledge therefore is the truth. It is the master plan
from the master architect. It is from the heart of God. It is a word that
is essential and addresses life at its source for our well-being. In order
to experience that well-being, a word of wisdom is needed to provide
direction as to how that word of knowledge is to be applied so that it
will bring the greatest blessings.

The addition of wisdom to knowledge is immensely valuable in many
aspects of life. An example of knowledge without wisdom from everyday
life is when a medical doctor tells a patient, "Our tests show you have
cancer and it is serious." Not to add a word of encouragement and tell
the person about some hopeful solution would lead to despair.

In counseling it is one thing to say to an individual, "I believe you
have some feelings of bitterness toward your mother." That is a word
of knowledge. It may well be the truth. But how does one change from
bitterness to forgiveness? A word of wisdom might suggest confession,
absolution, and other appropriate counsel that would empower the
person to be set free from the bitterness.

These examples show how important it is to have a helpful and
practical word of wisdom along with a word of knowledge so the individual is not left hanging without hope.

The word of knowledge and the word of wisdom work through our
intelligence and understanding. God uses those natural gifts which we
already have and which he has already given us, but we need to surrender
what we have in order to allow God to use us and manifest himself.
God is a perfect gentleman; he does not force anything on anyone
which they do not desire. So we need to make our faculties available
for the Spirit of God to use.

This means that the Spirit, through God's grace, inspires a person to proclaim a truth and see things and circumstances from the same perspective that God sees them. When this individual has yielded to the Spirit of God in this way, he or she is empowered to speak them to others so they also come to such a point.

We see an example of the word of wisdom when Jesus as a twelve-year-old was in the temple sitting among the teachers. This seems like a time in the life of a child when we do not expect much in terms of maturity. But we read that they "were amazed at his understanding" (LUKE 2:47). Apparently something unusual had taken place in the life of this boy of twelve. He had come to an understanding of truth as it was revealed by God and shared it with those in the temple. They also came to share in that word of wisdom—a practical and relevant word that amazed them. It was a word of knowledge that went beyond merely an exchange of facts and became wisdom that was relevant and useful for their lives.

An example of a word of knowledge would be when Jesus confronted the rich young man with the law stating, "You know the commandments" (MARK 10:19). This was the truth. It was truth that the young man already knew. The deeper truth is that God should come first. He knew the truth but did not apply it in his life. He had come to Jesus with a simple question, "Good Teacher, what must I do to inherit eternal life?" We can speculate about his motivation. The root problem may have been self-righteousness, idolatry, materialism, or pride. The problem was dealt with in a word of knowledge revealing the truth which was the law but was followed by a practical application of the law which was a word of wisdom. "Go, sell what you own, and give the money to the poor, and you will have treasure in heaven; then come, follow me" (MARK 10:21). Jesus in his wisdom and love cut through externals, reached down to the very root of this man's problem, and dealt with it. He saw a man who had a deeper problem; his god was his possessions. A word of knowledge was followed by a word of wisdom with specific practical application. Unfortunately, the man did not receive it and "went away grieving" (MARK 10:22).

Another example would be when Peter addressed the council in Jerusalem stating that the Gentiles should not follow the full law of Moses. This was an utterance of wisdom. Much of Paul's teaching in 1 Corinthians 12-14 is an utterance of wisdom, a practical application of the Word of God.

There is a difference between what we know through the natural process of learning and Spirit-inspired knowledge and wisdom. The Spirit of God touches our spirit in a way that natural learning cannot do, simply because it is a "manifestation" of the Spirit of Christ within a person. It makes a deep and unexplainable impact. It is a phenomenon that goes beyond the ordinary. It is Spirit touching spirit, whereas the natural can only touch the natural. For this reason Paul states,

> Those who are unspiritual do not receive the gifts of God's Spirit, for they are foolishness to them, and they are unable to understand them because they are spiritually discerned (1 COR. 2:14).

I have been present when someone has shared a word of knowledge or wisdom. It may not necessarily have been a completely new truth. But when it was completed, I felt that I had been in the presence of God.

The word for discerning of spirits (v. 10) also comes from two Greek words. The first word is *dia* meaning "through," "by means of," "by," or "with." The second word, *krino*, means "to separate," "to judge," "to sentence," "to decide," or "to determine." It belongs to the knowledge and wisdom family but it is a gift for determining the source of something.

In the discerning of spirits, Christianity teaches three negative sources of origin. Luther referred to them as the devil, the world, and the flesh. Discerning of spirits is a specific gift that gives people insight for determining whether what is spoken, said, or done is from the Lord or from some other source.

This experience into the gifts of deeper insight requires that we learn how to surrender our thoughts so that we can yield our mind to the Spirit of God, touching the very heart of God. As we from time to time reach such dimensions, the Spirit of God through grace gives us privileges and blessings beyond our fondest expectations.

Signs-and-Wonders Gifts

The next gifts that Paul mentions in this group will be referred to as the signs-and-wonders gifts: faith, gifts of healing, and the working of miracles. These gifts manifest the power of God in ways that often leave us mystified.

The words found at the end of Mark speak about some of the signs-and-wonders gifts. These words (MARK 16:9-20), however, are suspect. There are few, if any, scholars who consider the section to have been written by Mark. It is likely that someone later added it as an editorial comment or an attempt to improve on Mark's writing. Nevertheless, whoever wrote this bit of information attempted to tell us about God's way of confirming the truth of the message of the gospel:

> Go into all the world and preach the good news to all creation. Whoever believes and is baptized will be saved; but whoever does not believe will be condemned. And these signs will accompany those who believe: In my name they will drive out demons; they will speak in new tongues; they will pick up snakes with their hands; and when they drink deadly poison, it will not hurt them at all; they will place their hands on sick people, and they will get well (MARK 16:15-18 NIV).

The question of authorship does not detract from the emphasis the text is seeking to convey. This same emphasis was characteristic of the teaching of Jesus and Paul. Jesus sent out his disciples with the "keys of the kingdom" so that whatever they bound was bound and whatever they loosed was loosed (MATT. 16:18-19).

The specific objective of these signs-and-wonders gifts was to confirm the message of the gospel: "Jesus Christ is the same yesterday and today and forever" (HEB. 13:8).

The first gift in this category mentioned in 1 Corinthians 12:9 is the gift of faith. This gift of faith is different from the faith that assures our salvation. In *A Greek English Lexicon of the New Testament* (Chicago: University of Chicago Press, 1957, p. 669), we read,

> In addition to the faith (*pistis*) that every Christian possesses Paul speaks of a special gift of faith that is the possession of a select few 1 Corinthians 12:9. In this category he understands faith (*pistis*) as an unquestioning belief in God's power to aid men with miracles, the faith that "moves mountains." This special kind of faith is what the disciples had in mind when they asked "Increase our faith" (LUKE 17:5).

The gift of faith for salvation is also a special gift, but it does not seem to be related to the works of the Spirit as associated with the charismata. This is apparent in many portions of Scripture (EPH. 2:8). The gift of faith mentioned in the charismata seems to be a specific gift bestowed at a given time when there is a specific need to go beyond the limits of the ordinary. It is the kind of faith of which Christ was referring when he said,

> Truly, I tell you, if you say to this mountain, "Be taken up and thrown into the sea," and if you do not doubt in your heart, but believe that what you say will come to pass, it will be done for you. So I tell you, whatever you ask for in prayer, believe that you have received it, and it will be yours (MARK 11:23-24).

This gift of faith is a God-given confidence that persists and produces extraordinary results. The person who exudes this faith knows through the work of the Spirit in him or her that what is asked for will be given.

This kind of faith was evident in the prophet Elijah when he confronted the prophets of Baal and challenged them to a test. Whoever could produce the necessary results would prove to be the real God. Elijah proceeded to drench the offering to his God with water so as to make it even more difficult to ignite. A clear demonstration of the power of God was soon displayed before all the prophets of Baal. It is one thing to move out in foolishness, but it is another thing to have faith that the results that have been predicted will occur. Elijah had more than good intentions; he had a gift of faith that traced itself to the very presence of God.

It is apparent that people are not able to manipulate themselves into showing spectacular results from faith. This kind of faith demonstrates power that is unusual and extraordinary. It does not lend itself to rational explanation. The gift of faith spoken of here is a mighty manifestation of the power of God.

We now focus our attention on the other two gifts, namely, healings and working of miracles (1 COR. 12:9-10). Their close relationship is obvious. We need to point out that these gifts do not come at the beginning of this list where some would like to have them. Rather they are in the middle. Did Paul do this intentionally? There are many who want healing apart from Christ, the healer, and who want miracles without Christ, the miracle worker. The healing and the miracle apart from Jesus are, in essence, not possible. Jesus is the miracle and Jesus is the healer. No real healing or miracle can occur apart from Jesus.

It is interesting to note that the word for healing is in the plural (*himation*-genitive plural). Actually it is a double plural and ought to be literally translated "gifts of healings." What that seems to say is that God the healer keeps his options open. There is no specific way that God heals. God heals in various ways. He utilizes the gifts of doctors, physicians, surgeons. He utilizes the gifts of medications and therapies to enable the process of healing. But neither physicians nor medications heal. It is Jesus who heals. The Lord may choose to heal without doctors, surgeons, or medication. He may choose to heal in ways that are completely foreign to us. The Lord needs to be the focus, not the healing or the way it is accomplished.

In this respect God may choose to heal someone in a manner that is foreign to the accepted practices that we rely on so readily. Systematizing a specific method invariably ends up in fruitlessness. God is a God of variety and the true working of the Spirit never is limited to one specific method through which people are healed.

It is interesting to study how Jesus healed people. About the time we think that we have pinned down his method we find him using another. At times he laid hands on the sick. At others he proceeded to make a spittle of clay. Sometimes he told the sick to stand and walk. Sometimes they merely touched the hem of his garment. But whatever means he employed, through his power, people were healed. The lepers were cleansed "as they went" (LUKE 17:14).

These signs-and-wonders gifts were given to "all of them in everyone" (1 COR. 12:7). They are given to the body of Christ to convey the grace of God to God's people so that they might experience the love of God in Christ in new ways. This seems to be clear from the question raised and the answer given in James.

> Are any among you sick? They should call for the elders of the church and have them pray over them, anointing them with oil in the name of the Lord. The prayer of faith will save the sick, and the Lord will raise them up; and anyone who has committed sins will be forgiven (JAMES 5:14-15).

The direction given is that the sick should call for the specific selected leaders (elders in this case) in a specific body of believers (their church).

They are to pray and anoint with oil in the name of the Lord Jesus. There is no specific directive to seek out one specific individual with the gift of healing, but to trust the Spirit of God "who allots to each one individually just as the Spirit chooses" (1 COR. 12:11).

In the spiritual gift described as "workings of miracles," we are confronted with a manifestation of God's power at its fullest. The literal translation of miracles is really "in-workings of power, of dynamic, of energy" (*energemata*—a nominative plural, or *dunameon*—a genitive plural). The interesting thing is that this gift is listed separately when actually all the gifts have a miraculous nature. The gift takes on the nature of mysterious energy or power.

This gift is not limited to one specific area such as healing, but is present in various areas, such as deliverance, the casting out of demons, receiving something desperately needed from an unknown source, raising people from the dead, and receiving help to escape from danger. This gift includes any manifestation that is beyond ordinary human ability.

Such manifestations are implied in a number of places in reference to Paul; for example, "God did extraordinary miracles through Paul" (ACTS 19:11). It is also written, "Stephen, full of grace and power, did great wonders and signs among the people" (ACTS 6:8). The people of Samaria were impressed with the signs and miracles that were performed by Philip (ACTS 8:5-8).

We must always remember that the miraculous on occasion manifests itself through the natural. We see a good example in the life of Paul. Frequently he was exposed to trials where he needed something miraculous, but it did not manifest itself immediately. Instead the need was met at later times. In the story of the shipwreck on Malta, natural circumstances, and not a miraculous manifestation, brought Paul and the rest to shore. They floated to shore on planks and debris. It was only after they were on shore when Paul was bitten by a snake that something miraculous occurred and his life was saved (ACTS 27:39—28:6).

The power of God poured out at Pentecost on the early Christians (ACTS 2) did not render them all supernatural powers to perform miracles. Always in the life of the Christian there is a blending of the natural with the supernatural.

Word Gifts

Prophecy (1 COR. 12:10) is at the heart of Pentecost. When the Pentecost experience was taking place, Peter said,

This is what was spoken through the prophet Joel: "In the last days it will be, God declares, that I will pour out my Spirit upon all flesh, and your sons and your daughters shall prophesy, and your young men shall see visions, and your old men shall dream dreams. Even upon my slaves, both men and women, in those days I will pour out my Spirit; and they shall prophesy. And I will show portents in the heaven above and signs on the earth below" (ACTS 2:16-19).

Prophecy is the only gift listed three times: as an office gift, a personality gift, and also as a manifestational gift. This indicates its importance. We should be not surprised that the wise sage wrote in Proverbs 29:18, "Where there is no prophecy, the people cast off restraint" (NRSV) or "Where there is no vision, the people perish" (KJV).

We need to provide some information about the roots of the word *prophecy* in the Proverbs passage. The term used for prophecy in Proverbs 29:18 is the word *chazon*. It is not the most frequently used term for prophet in the Old Testament. The most frequently used word is *nabyiah*. However *chazon* is also a term that is listed under other terms for prophet in the *Theological Dictionary of the New Testament*.

The term *chazon* is used at least thirty-five times in the Old Testament, including 1 Samuel 3:1.

In the early period of Samuel there was no *chazon* and therefore no word of God. What is granted to Samuel is such a *chazon*; he is summoned during the night and receives a message from God. This, however, makes him a *nabi* [prophet] (v. 20). It appears therefore that in this period, when the tribes of Israel borrowed so much from their neighbors, that nabis also adopted the "method" of *chazon* as a means of revelation. In like manner, the absence of *chazon*, i.e., the absence of divine revelation, is later interpreted as the ruin of the people (Proverbs 29:18) (*Theological Dictionary of the Old Testament*, vol. 4, Grand Rapids: Wm. B. Eerdmans, 1980, p. 282, 285).

This explanation helps us understand to some extent why Paul states that we ought to "earnestly desire the spiritual gifts, especially that you may prophesy" (1 COR. 14:1 RSV). From all these passages it is apparent that prophecy is a very important gift for the ongoing work of the kingdom of God.

What is prophesying? Much information has been given about it under office gifts and personality gifts. Essentially the prophet is a person who brings a message from the Lord. Often this has been associated with preaching and teaching. Preaching and teaching may be prophetic or they may not. It depends on whether what is preached is from the heart of God or not. Some preaching is prophetic in that what is proclaimed becomes a reality. Ultimately, that which is proclaimed as a Word from God must be confirmed by reality.

The guiding mark of prophecy—whether it comes to us through an office gift, a personality gift, or a manifestational gift—is that it is a message from God. In the book of Haggai this idea is expressed quite clearly: "Then Haggai, the messenger of the Lord, spoke to the people with the Lord's message, saying, 'I am with you,' says the Lord" (Hag. 1:13).

The prophetic word is important in a day when people are tired of hearing the opinions of people who have nothing to confirm their authority as a word from the heart of God. God's people long to hear a clear and precise word from the Lord that confirms and is in harmony with the Bible. Without a proper word from the Lord there is no clear sense of direction. Our deeper need is that we respect the prophetic gift so that a proper and clear message may be brought to the entire church. This will enable the church to be the salt of the earth and light of the world.

We need to be alert to the manifestation of this gift as it surfaces from time to time through various members of the body of Christ. After all, prophets were second to the apostles and, as mentioned before, are included in the foundation of the household of God (EPH. 2:20).

But it was also apparent in the early church that because many prophesied, there needed to be some limitations to the number who spoke. The others were encouraged to weigh what was being prophesied in order to determine whether it was a word from the Lord. Since we are all sinners and no one is perfect, it is quite possible that a prophetic word can be uttered in the flesh so that it is not a word from the Lord at all. As Ezekiel said, They "prophesy out of their own imagination. . . . follow their own spirit" (EZEK. 13:2-3).

For this reason Paul encouraged only two or three to speak and the others to weigh what was spoken. Any person who is led to proclaim a prophetic word must also have the humility to have it weighed by members of the body of Christ. Furthermore, the person must also have the humility to accept from time to time that it may not be considered to be a word from the Lord at all or perhaps only meant for the individual that brought the word.

The specific purpose of a prophetic word was for "upbuilding and encouragement and consolation" (1 COR. 14:3). From all the examples that we find in Scripture, we discover that prophets were not all that popular. Basically that was because they frequently had to bring a word that people did not wish to hear. Prophets are inclined to call a sin a sin. Frequently, prophets and prophecies are rejected because they involve dealing with some sin. It becomes immensely important that every prophecy be prayerfully given and received, or prayerfully weighed and rejected if found to be a word that is not from the Lord. The first test for an authentic prophetic word is that it must always be in harmony with the Word of God.

The next word gift that is mentioned is tongues and the interpretation of tongues (1 COR. 12:10). These gifts more than any others have caused confusion and disharmony in the body of Christ. So much has been written that some may think that the gift of tongues is the only charisma. Much of the confusion and debate centers in the teaching by classical pentecostals that the initial sign or substantiating evidence of the baptism of the Holy Spirit is a manifestation of tongues. Most other charismatics do not agree on this, and so the debate continues.

The Spirit of God is poured out upon us already at baptism. Furthermore, God in his love does not force anything on people that they do not desire, but tongues and interpretation are also legitimate gifts. It is interesting that they are mentioned last in this group of gifts. For some this provides a reason to exclude them entirely. But we need to admit that they were also included. Therefore, these must also be legitimate gifts for all God's people and "All these are activated by one and the same Spirit" (1 COR. 12:11). What then are these specific gifts? What is the purpose and how are they used properly so they do not cause endless dissension and disharmony in the Christian church?

This gift is often referred to as glossolalia. This is another term that comes from a combination of two Greek words. The first word is tongue, speech, talk (glossa). The second word is babble, talk, speak, utter (laleo). When the two words are combined, we have the word glossolalia: "speaking in tongues."

Glossolalia is a gift that is bestowed on a person by the Spirit of God. It is not usually understood by the one who speaks but needs interpretation by one who has the gift of interpretation. At times an individual may have both the gift of speaking and interpretation. Glossolalia is a kind of speech that is inspired and directed by the Spirit of God. The effects of glossolalia are more interior than exterior.

Frequently the focus is on what is heard rather than what is experienced. Glossolalia is not like a learned language that has specific characteristics of expression by which it communicates meaning. The speaker does not consciously decide what is to be stated in terms of words. This gift does not usually lend itself to rational thinking and understanding. There have been instances when an individual has spoken in a tongue and another has recognized it to be a specific foreign language, but in those cases, it was not a language the individual had learned. Such an experience is the exception, not the rule.

Glossolalia is a gift that needs to be received by faith. It is a gift that needs to be expressed in faith. It comes under the category of childlikeness. As Jesus said,

> Truly I tell you, unless you change and become like children, you will never enter the kingdom of heaven. Whoever becomes humble like this child is the greatest in the kingdom of heaven (MATT. 18:3-4).

In the verses prior to this passage Jesus was asked a question related to greatness in the kingdom of heaven. The answer was one of being childlike and practicing humility as a little child. It requires a great deal of humility to babble like a little child when experiencing the gift of glossolalia. But even as the Father in heaven understands the babbling of a little child, so the Father also understands the Spirit-inspired babbling of an adult who yields his or her mind and tongue to the Lord to bring glory and honor to God's name.

The gift of glossolalia is mentioned only in Mark, Acts, and 1 Corinthians. In Mark and Acts it was given as a sign that people were believers in Christ or that the Holy Spirit had come upon them (MARK 16:17, ACTS 2:4; 10:46; 19:6). In Acts 2:4, glossolalia seems to have been an ability to speak in a foreign language without having learned that language.

In 1 Corinthians we read that this gift had a different kind of emphasis. It was given as a type of private praying for personal inspiration and edification. When glossolalia is used in harmony with the gift of interpretation, it does become a gift that is useful to the body of Christ. The basic purpose for this gift is for building up the individual believer and is specifically suited for private devotions and meditation. Most individuals in charismatic renewal hardly ever utilize this gift in public, but instead use it in their own devotional time in prayer, praise, and intercession.

There are two different ways in which tongues are utilized to glorify God. The first is the most frequent, and that is to use this gift as a private form of devotion for praying and praising God. It is yielding oneself to the Spirit of God in a very humble and childlike faith so that God in his love can enable a deeper kind of prayer which goes beyond ordinary mental processes.

The second kind of expression in tongues is in a public forum or service. When a tongue is manifested in a public service, there is always an expectation of interpretation. As is the case with prophecy, such a word always needs to be weighed by other Christians to discern its authenticity. This might best be done by a group of individuals, such as a specifically designated leadership with spiritual maturity. Another much less common public expression is sometimes found at certain kinds of charismatic worship gathering when all, in unrehearsed manner, begin singing in tongues. Each one sings in his or her own tongue in a type of melodious expression that resembles a symphony, with the sounds blending together in beautiful harmony and praise. It is not a single voice speaking out which would require interpretation, but it is rather an expression of individual tongues singing together in an expression of praise to God. In times past it has been called "jubilate" or "jubilation" and historically was practiced by many Christians. Ralph Martin tells us,

> Numbers of music historians, in their attempts to understand the roots of Western music, have researched the common practice of congregations and individual Christians of this period using wordless singing as a means of praising God. Most of the Church Fathers laud this practice. Jubilation (L. jubili— shouts or sounds of joy), "wordless praise," "wordless psalms," and the "singing of alleluia," were some of the terms used to

describe this singing of wordless hymns. Augustine, perhaps, defines it best. He states that Jubilation is a breaking forth into a singing of vowel sounds. He furthermore states: "What is jubilation? Joy that cannot be expressed in words; yet the voice expresses what is conceived within and cannot be explained in words: this is jubilation. . . . He who sings a jubilus does not utter words: he pronounces a wordless sound of joy; the voice of his soul pours forth happiness as intensely as possible, expressing what he feels without reflecting on any particular meaning. To manifest his joy the man does not use words that can be pronounced and understood, but he simply lets his joy burst forth without words; his voice then appears to express a happiness so intense that he cannot formulate it" (Emar. in Ps. 94,3; 99,4). . . . Jubilation, in a free, improvised Spirit-led form appears to have been a major part of the life of the Christian Church at least till the first part of the seventh century (*Hungry for God*, Garden City, N.Y.: Doubleday & Co., 1971, pp. 165–66).

Since jubilation is basically a group expression of praise, it is generally thought to need no interpretation. However, words of Scripture and prophecy usually follow after a time of singing in tongues.

Glossolalia often served as a sign that the Spirit of God had been received, as we read in the book of Acts (ACTS 10:45-46; 19:6). But there does not appear to be any substantiating evidence that two different kinds of glossolalia exist, one as an indication that the infilling of the Spirit had taken place and the other a type of charismatic gift. The same term is used with little variation. It is again one of those mysteries where we see the Spirit of God utilizing a gift in different ways to accomplish specific purposes.

As the gift of healing does not use one specific or uniform technique, so the gift of tongues does not lend itself to being boxed in, evaluated, or dissected to satisfy our rational minds.

This gift needs to be properly used. If any gift is overemphasized or abused, it may readily become an idol. In that case, the gift becomes more important than the giver. For this reason Paul wrote to the Corinthians. They had abused this gift of glossolalia. He did not reprimand them for using the gift, but only for abusing the gift. Paul says,

I thank God that I speak in tongues more than all of you; nevertheless, in church I would rather speak five words with my mind, in order to instruct others also, than ten thousand words in a tongue (1 COR. 14:18-19).

He did not tell them to discontinue using this gift, but only to use it properly. The solution to abuse is not disuse, but proper use. To ignore this or any gift is only to force those expressing it to feel different and sometimes defensive, and dissension is the result. When recognized as a gift that has proper place for expression when done "decently and in order" (1 COR. 14:40), then it becomes a blessing. However, when it is ignored, discouraged, or misused, it has a way of becoming the means for disharmony and disunity.

QUESTIONS FOR DISCUSSION OR REFLECTION

1. How did this chapter's discussion help you to understand the difference between knowledge and wisdom?

2. Would it be selfish to want the sign-and-wonders gifts (faith, healings, workings of miracles)? Is it possible to be selective in what gifts we desire?

3. The gifts of prophecy, speaking in tongues, and interpretation of tongues have often been the most controversial. How can they be expressed or practiced so they become useful and upbuilding rather than divisive?

CHAPTER 6

The Fruit of the Spirit

GALATIANS 5:22-23

Someone once said that the basic test to determine whether someone is filled with the Spirit is not by evidence of the gifts but of the fruit. Jesus himself said,

> You will know them by their fruits. Are grapes gathered from thorns, or figs from thistles? In the same way, every good tree bears good fruit, but the bad tree bears bad fruit. A good tree cannot bear bad fruit, nor can a bad tree bear good fruit. Every tree that does not bear good fruit is cut down and thrown into the fire. Thus you will know them by their fruits (MATT. 7:16-20).

It is interesting to note that in Greek the word for fruit (*karpos*) is singular. This seems to imply that if a person has the Spirit, that individual is blessed with all the fruit.

The fruit of the Spirit seems like the normal result if a person is endowed with the Spirit of God. Where the Spirit of God is, we expect Christlikeness, Christian maturity, and godliness. Since all Christians have a responsibility to grow in their faith, they certainly also have the responsibility through the grace of God to develop the fruit of the Spirit so that it manifests itself in their lives in a humble manner. Fruit is not poured out as the gifts. Fruit is something that grows and develops as the individual in obedience learns to walk in yieldedness to the Spirit of God. In *Your Spiritual Gifts*, C. Peter Wagner says, "While spiritual gifts help define what a Christian does, the fruit of the Spirit helps define what a Christian is" (Ventura, Calif.: GL Publications, 1985, p. 89).

The fruit of the Spirit is basic for a proper use of the charismata. When Christians live by the fruit of the Spirit, there will surely be less likelihood of division and disharmony. Any gifts lacking proper expression or manifestation of the fruit are suspect if not useless. This was one of the basic problems in the church at Corinth where the people abused the gifts.

The gifts had become showpieces that were used to bring attention and honor, not to the Lord, but to the people who had them. They were busy using the gifts, but the more they used them, the more the gifts brought dissension and disharmony to the body of Christ. Paul wrote 1 Corinthians to admonish them of their pride and self-centeredness. They were what could be called "Spirit filled, Spirit baptized, Spirit anointed," but basically they were spiritual disasters. The basic problem was not in the gifts but in the way in which people used them to set themselves apart from others. Pride and self-centeredness caused division among them.

1 Corinthians 13 calls these people to demonstrate love and compassion, for without a proper expression of love they were nothing more than noisy gongs or clanging cymbals. Paul proceeds to elaborate on all the gifts they could possess, but says that if they did not have love, the first fruit named in Galatians 5:22, they were "nothing" (1 COR. 13:1-3). Gifts without fruit are something like a brand new car without gas. The car has all the potential for transportation and comfort, but it lacks the one basic ingredient that will enable it to fulfill its basic function.

Various attempts have been made to place the fruit into basic classifications. None are really satisfactory and all have strengths and weaknesses. Paul may not have intended for them to be categorized, but there is some logic in putting them in three basic categories, each category having three gifts. The first three—love, joy, and peace—deal basically with our relationship to God. The second three—patience, kindness, and goodness—deal with our relationship to others. The last three—faithfulness, gentleness, and self-control—deal with basic qualities that relate to ourselves.

Our Relationship With God

It is not only fitting but also logical that the first fruit mentioned is love (GAL. 5:22). We are reminded of Paul's words that tell us how powerfully God's love sustained the early Christians in their suffering:

> And not only that, but we also boast in our sufferings, knowing that suffering produces endurance, and endurance produces character, and character produces hope, and hope does not disappoint us, because God's love has been poured into our hearts through the Holy Spirit that has been given to us (ROM. 5:3-5).

We also remember the lawyer who came to Jesus somewhat arrogantly inquiring what was the most important commandment. Each of the parallel Gospel accounts agrees that the most important commandment is,

> "You shall love the Lord your God with all your heart, and with all your soul, and with all your mind." This is the greatest and first commandment. And a second is like it, "You shall love your neighbor as yourself" (MATT. 22:37-39; also MARK 12:30-34; LUKE 10:25-28).

There is some variation in each of the accounts. In Matthew we are informed that on these two commandments depend all "the law and the prophets," a reference to the Bible of that day. This at least infers that we can better understand what God intends for us when love for God and neighbor is not only stated but also practiced. The basic focus of all law and prophecy was love, love for God and love for neighbor. It is the very nature of God. "God is love" (1 John 4:16).

Mark 12:33 informs us that this commandment is much more than the "burnt offerings and sacrifices." To a Jew, burnt offerings and sacrifices meant a great deal because they were the basis for their forgiveness and salvation. It was their way of getting into the presence of God.

Luke is the most fascinating of all the parallel texts, and also somewhat frustrating. The question the lawyer asked Jesus was in reference to what he needed to do to inherit eternal life. Nearly anyone who has had even a meager bit of Sunday school and confirmation instruction would know that the answer would be John 3:16 or Romans 1:17. But words similar to them are not present in this text. Rather Jesus asked this lawyer what was written in the law. He responded with the commandment, "Love the Lord your God with all your heart, . . . and your neighbor as yourself" (LUKE 10:27-28). Again we would expect Jesus to correct him by telling him that his salvation rested in Jesus. But we are surprised to find that Jesus said, "You have given the right answer; do this, and you will live" (LUKE 10:28).

Obviously, there has to be something deeper than what appears on the surface. It seems that Jesus is saying that real and fulfilled living begins with love for God. Even faith in Christ begins with love and trust in God. Jesus seems to indicate that when the main focus becomes love for God, every other aspect of life also begins to fall into place. But love is also a gift. It is not something that we conjure up within us by sheer determination and will power. This we also recognize as a gift to us by the grace of God.

Ultimately, we begin to see that without love for God nothing else that is good is possible. Love for other members of the human family cannot take place apart from love for God. We can understand why Paul wrote to the Galatians and exhorted them, "Bear one another's burdens, and in this way you will fulfill the law of Christ" (GAL. 6:2).

There is no other way whereby we can fulfill the law of Christ apart from love to God and love to human beings. It is this love that the Spirit of God seeks to pour into the hearts of people.

Recently, a pastor from India stated that he noticed a difference in Americans from his previous visit some years ago. He felt that Americans had lost a certain amount of fear and respect for God. He said that since they have lost their fear of God, they have also lost some of the zeal they had displayed in their love for God. He went on to state that only as Americans begin to pray for restoration of both fear and love for God will they once again come to experience the power of God. His words seem to be worth our while to consider. Perhaps we are too close to our circumstances to discern what needs to be changed.

The love for God that we experience as a result of God's love for us has a dynamic influence on our entire outlook on life. Our attitude completely changes. We begin to look at people and life around us from a different perspective. We discover new meaning and purpose for life and living. Our love for God gives us a positive attitude in our relationship with God and our relationship with spouse, family, and others in our lives. This mysterious, motivating dynamic keeps us moving in righteousness and holiness. Yet it also provides a proper balance in our lives, keeping us from those things that bring disharmony into our lives and others'. This dynamic of love for God touches us in such a way that we are not only loving, but also peaceful and joyful.

Love has many by-products. Love manifests itself in various ways, one of them in the joy that is experienced when we are loved. Joy is presented in the Bible as being essential for our well-being: "A joyful heart is good medicine, but a downcast spirit dries up the bones" (PROV. 17:22 RSV).

The word in Greek for joys is *chara*. It is a word that has a quality all its own. It is a word that is used selectively in the New Testament. It is a word that has its roots in a spirituality whose foundation is in God the Father as revealed in Christ. This *chara* is not a joy which momentarily bursts forth, nor is it a joy that comes from an accumulation of material things. Neither is it a joy that comes because we have been triumphant over another individual or cause. Such misconceptions of joy can be quite disillusioning.

Many often miss the true joy in life because society frequently gives the impression that joy can only come through prestige, popularity, or an accumulation of material things. It is immensely disillusioning to discover after the accumulation that nothing has changed in life. This misconception leads to even more joylessness.

Chara is a joy that has its roots in a manifestation of the Spirit of God. The Spirit of God reveals to us the love of the Father through his Son. Scripture testifies to this again and again. It states that God has no pleasure in the sadness of the spirit but desires that we be joyful in him. The mission of his Son was not to make people miserable, but to provide the basis for a joyful and abundant life. So it is that we find that the prophets, apostles, and Christ himself not only admonish but also command us to be joyful in such passages as:

Make a joyful noise to God (PS. 66:1; also 81:1; 95:1-2; 98:4; 100:1).

Rejoice in the Lord always; and again I will say, Rejoice (PHIL. 4:4).

But rejoice insofar as you are sharing Christ's sufferings, so that you may also be glad and shout for joy when his glory is revealed (1 PET. 4:13).

Luther compared this loving, joyful experience to the relationship of a bridegroom and his bride. A bride and groom who have fallen in love with each other exhibit the natural by-product of such love: the overflowing joy which emanates from their lives. Their life together is a continual manifestation of joy in all that they do. Even the mundane things become opportunities of joy.

A person who has truly experienced the love, grace, mercy, and forgiveness of the Father through Christ will naturally radiate with joy in the midst of all kinds of circumstance. Jesus is frequently referred to as the groom, and we—the church, the body of Christ—as the bride. The manifestation of joy is one of the natural characteristics of all who have experienced the outpouring of the Spirit of God in their lives. We read of this in the life of Paul:

> We are putting no obstacle in anyone's way, so that no fault may be found with our ministry, but as servants of God we have commended ourselves in every way: through great endurance, in afflictions, hardship, calamities, beatings, imprisonments, riots, labors, sleepless nights, hunger; by purity, knowledge, patience, kindness, holiness of spirit, genuine love, truthful speech, and the power of God; with the weapons of righteousness for the right hand and for the left; in honor and dishonor, in ill repute and good repute. We are treated as impostors, and yet are true; as unknown, and yet are well known; as dying, and see—we are alive; as punished, and yet not killed; as sorrowful, *yet always rejoicing*; as poor, yet making many rich; as having nothing, and *yet possessing everything* (2 COR. 6:3-10).

Another by-product of love is peace. The original Greek word for peace is *irene*. In casual and informal conversation this word had two meanings. One was the experience a nation enjoyed during a time when it lived in harmony with its neighbors, when a village had kept the peace through proper order. However, in biblical usage, peace went beyond this meaning. It does not mean only that we are free from strife and trouble, but that we have the good pleasure to appropriate for our lives that which is the best.

People everywhere—in every nation, in every religion, in every walk of life—long for peace. Politicians lull us to sleep with campaign proclamations of peace only to disillusion us with much less than peace after they take office. Peace marches, peace organizations, and peace movements all proclaim their objective to be peace, but in the midst of all their activity and rhetoric they often stir up disharmony and fail to achieve peace.

But this *irene* (peace) listed as fruit of the Spirit is more of a subjective virtue. It is a quietness that we experience within ourselves. It is the exact opposite of anxiety and fear. It is the quiet calm that comes upon people who know that all is well between them and the Father. For they have come to know the Savior in a most intimate way. They know without a shadow of doubt they are forgiven and that all is well with their souls.

It is like the man who was dying from lung cancer. He made it quite clear to me at the very outset that he was not a Christian. When I asked him if I could pray with him after the doctor had told him in my presence that he had terminal cancer, he said, "I am not a praying man and I am not about to start now." Somewhat surprised, I responded, "Well, I guess I can understand that if you have never prayed, you might feel uncomfortable praying now, but could I have the privilege to visit with you again?" He said, "Sure, I wouldn't mind."

I committed myself to visit with him each week, even though he was not a member of our congregation. I called on him for months, never asking him to pray with me. I only sought to bring Jesus to him in some way through my presence. One day he called and asked to be baptized. I came and shared the gospel with him. He made a confession of faith in Jesus Christ as Lord and Savior. His cancer continued to spread even though we faithfully prayed for his physical healing. His condition continued to deteriorate until he went into a coma.

One night the family called me to come as it appeared the end was imminent. I rushed to the hospital to discover that he had come out of the coma. When I walked into the room he said, "Hello, Pastor, I am so glad to see you." I said, "How are you?" He responded without hesitation, "Just great, just great." I inquired, "But how is it with your soul?" He responded, "Just great, just great, tell my family, the Lord may not have healed me physically, but he sure healed me spiritually."

I asked him, "Do you have peace with the Lord?" With a smile he said, "Yes, Pastor, I have peace." Shortly after that, he once again slipped into a coma and with a smile on his lips he died. This is the kind of peace these verses describe:

> Rejoice in the Lord always; again I will say, Rejoice. Let your gentleness be known to everyone. The Lord is near. Do not worry about anything, but in everything by prayer and supplication with thanksgiving let your requests be made known to God. And the peace of God, which surpasses all understanding, will guard your hearts and your minds in Christ Jesus (PHIL. 4:4-7).

> Now may the Lord of peace himself give you peace at all times in all ways. The Lord be with all of you (2 THESS. 3:16).

> "Peace I leave with you; my peace I give to you. I do not give to you as the world gives. Do not let your hearts be troubled, and do not let them be afraid" (JOHN 14:27).

John R. W. Stott writes about these first three qualities:

> The Holy Spirit puts God's love in our hearts, God's joy in our souls and God's peace in our minds. Love, joy and peace pervade a Spirit-filled Christian. Indeed, these may be said to be his principal and abiding characteristics. Everything he does is conceived in love, undertaken with joy and accomplished in peace (*Baptism and Fullness*, Downers Grove, Ill.: Inter Varsity Press, 1971, p. 77).

Our Relationship with Others

The relationship of love, joy, and peace with God has a positive impact on our relationship with others. This brings us to the second group of fruit: patience, kindness, and goodness (GAL. 5:22 RSV).

Patience is a character quality that waits and waits and then is able to wait some more. The Greek word for patience (*makrothumia*) is an interesting word. It is stated that the Romans became world conquerors simply because they had the quality of patient persistence. They would not make peace with an enemy even when defeated. It was a conquering type of patience. In the Bible, a more peaceful kind of patience is intended.

In the New Testament, patience is used to describe the attitude of God with his people as we read,

> Or do you despise the riches of his kindness and forbearance and patience? Do you not realize that God's kindness is meant to lead you to repentance (ROM. 2:4)?

If God had been like us in our sinful nature, he would have eliminated us a long time ago and started over. But God has the quality of patience that keeps loving until there is a response.

The words *kindness* and *goodness* (also translated generosity) are closely related to patience. Patience manifests itself in actions that are kind and good. Patience does not take revenge but rather seeks ways through which to express itself in kindness and goodness. Kindness and goodness are inherent characteristics of patience. Patience blended with them cannot retaliate. It is a quality with which we can pray for the blessing and mercy of God for our enemy. It helps us serve God's people in concrete and constructive ways. Patience, kindness, and goodness seem to be steps that move upward on the scale of Christian maturity in our relationship with Christ and others.

Our Relationship with Ourselves

Finally we come to the last three fruit-bearing qualities: faithfulness, gentleness, and self-control (GAL. 5:22-23). The word for faithfulness can be translated by the word *trustworthiness*. At other times it might be translated to mean "reliable." The implied meaning here is not a faith that relies on the Lord, but rather how reliable, trustworthy, and faithful we might be.

The second word goes beyond the meaning of gentleness as we understand it in English. It also means to be submissive to the will of God. It means to be able to receive from others so as to learn. It is a kind of humility that knows that it does not know everything.

Basically, gentleness is a word that demonstrates consideration to others. It is a character quality that surfaces from an individual who is living in close fellowship with God. It is not a quality of the anemic and weak but of those strong in the Spirit.

The last of this triad—self-control—is the quality of mastering self. It is a discipline able to say "yes" at the proper time and "no" at the proper time. It is not influenced by public opinion.

Self-control was a quality of Greek rulers who supposedly never let their private affairs have any influence on their governmental decisions. Self-control is the fruit that enables people to be so totally in control over their own desires that they are able to be servants to others.

Paul believed that when people became Christians they died with Christ and rose with Christ (ROM. 6:1-11). When they rose, they rose to a new life in which the lust of the flesh and the pride of life were gone. In this new life the beautiful things of the Spirit of God that were within them would radiate out through their lives in Christlikeness and holiness.

The charismata are not the end. Rather, the fruit of the Spirit makes the charismata attractive, effective, and productive. The fruit of the Spirit, present in the lives of believers, can touch the hearts and lives of people and draw them to the mercy of God in Christ Jesus. Love, joy, peace, patience, kindness, goodness, faithfulness, gentleness, and self-control enable effective witness and ministry. We need to pray for guidance about our gifts and the gifts of others. But more specifically we need to pray for an increase in the fruit of the Spirit in our lives so we do not simply become proud, arrogant, empty gongs and clanging cymbals. As we, by the grace of God, discover and utilize the gifts God has given us and as we by his grace radiate with the fruit of the Spirit, multitudes will long to know Jesus, for they will also desire to be a part of a body which radiates with such grace and mercy.

QUESTIONS FOR DISCUSSION OR REFLECTION

1. Why is it natural that a close and intimate relationship with God through Jesus will reveal a manifestation of love, joy, and peace in our lives?

2. Patience, kindness, and goodness are not easy to practice. What experiences in your life have helped you to become more patient, kind, and good?

3. We may wish our lives to demonstrate more faithfulness, gentleness, and self-control. Which values, practices, and temptations in our culture have a tendency to push us in the opposite direction from these? What can we do to radiate with the "fruit of the Spirit" in our lives?

BIBLIOGRAPHY

ABBOTT, T. K. *The International Critical Commentary*, "Epistles to the Ephesians and Colossians." New York: Scribner and Sons, 1916.

ALLEN, Willoughby C. *The International Critical Commentary*. Edinburgh: T and T Clark, 1955.

BARCLAY, William. *The Letter to the Corinthians*. Philadelphia: The Westminister Press, 1956.

BARTH, Markus. *Ephesians 4-6*. Garden City: Doubleday and Company, 1978.

BAUER, Arndt and Gingrich. *Greek English Lexicon of the New Testament*. Chicago: University of Chicago Press, 1957.

BEYER, Herman W., *Diakoneo, Theological Dictionary of the New Testament*.

BONHOEFFER, Dietrich. *Life Together*. New York: Harper and Brothers, 1954.

BOTTERWECK, G. J., and Ringgren, Helmer. *Theological Dictionary of the New Testament*. Translated by David Green. Grand Rapids, Michigan: William Eerdmans Publishing Co., 1980.

BRUNER, Frederick. *A Theology of the Holy Spirit*. Grand Rapids, Michigan: Eerdmans Publishing Co., 1982.

BUECHSEL, Friedrich. *Didasko, Theological Dictionary of the New Testament*.

BULTMANN, Rudolf. *Ginosko, Theological Dictionary of the New Testament*.

CHRISTENSON, Larry, ed. *Welcome, Holy Spirit*. Minneapolis: Augsburg Publishing House, 1987.

CONZELMAN, Hans. *An Outline of the Theology of the New Testament*. New York: Harper and Row, 1968.

CRUDEN, Alexander A. M. *Cruden's Complete Concordance*. Grand Rapids, Michigan: Zondervan Publishing House, 1949.

DIBELIUS, Martin. *Commentary on the Epistle of James*. Philadelphia: Fortress Press.

ERICKSON, Stanford C. *The Essence of Good Teaching*. San Francisco: Jassey-Bass Publishers, 1984

FORDE, Gerhard. "Forensic Justification and Law in Lutheran Theology." *Justification by Faith*. Edited by H. George Anderson, T. Austin Murphy, and Joseph A. Burgess. Minneapolis: Augsburg Publishing Co., 1985.

FRIEDRICH, Gerhard, *Prophetes, Theological Dictionary of the New Testament*.

GREEK LEXICON. New York: Harper and Brothers.

GREEN, Thomas H., S. J. *When the Well Runs Dry*. Notre Dame, Indiana: Ave Maria Press, 1985.

HALS, Ronald M. *Grace and Faith in the Old Testament*. Minneapolis: Augsburg Publishing Co., 1980.

KAESEMANN, Ernest. *Commentary on Romans*. Grand Rapids: William Eerdmans Publishing Co., 1982.

KILDAHL, John P. *The Psychology of Speaking in Tongues*. New York: Harper and Row Publishers, Inc., 1972.

KOENIG, John. *Charismata: God's Gift for God's People*. Philadelphia: Westminster Press, 1972.

LAKOFF, George, and Johnson, Mark. *Metaphors We Live By*. Chicago and London: University of Chicago Press, 1980.

LOWMAN, Joseph. *Mastering the Techniques of Teaching*. San Francisco: Jassey-Bass Publishers, 1984.

LUTHER, Martin. *Commentary on the Epistle to the Romans*. Translated by J. Theodore Mueller. Grand Rapids, Michigan: Zondervan Publishing House.

LUTHER, Martin. *D. Martin Luthers Werke: Kritische Gesamtausgabe*. Vol. 35. Weimar: Hermann Böhlaus Verlag, 1964.

MCRAE, William J. *The Dynamics of Spiritual Gifts*. Grand Rapids, Michigan: Zondervan Publishing House, 1949.

MARTIN, Ralph. *Hungry for God*. Garden City, New York: Doubleday and Company, 1971.

MINNEAPOLIS STAR AND TRIBUNE. April 23, 1987.

PRENTER, Regin. *Spiritus Creator*. Philadelphia: Fortress Press, 1953.

PRIDIE, J. R. *The Spiritual Gifts*. London: Robert Scott.

REICKE, Bo, *Proistemi, Theological Dictionary of the New Testament*.

RENGSTORF, K. R., "Apostolos," in *Theological Dictionary of the New Testament*.

ROBINSON, J. A. *St. Paul's Epistle to the Ephesians*. London: Clark, 1922.

RYRIE, Charles Caldwell. *The Grace of God*. Chicago: Moody Press, 1963.

SCHUBERT, Leland. *Guide to Oral Communication*. New York: Prentice Hall, Inc., 1948.

SCHUTZ, John H. *Paul and the Anatomy of Apostolic Authority*. Cambridge: University Press, 1975.

SCHWEIZER, Eduard. "*Soma*," in *Theological Dictionary of the New Testament*.

SHARAN, Shlomo and Yael. *Small-Group Interaction*. Englewood Cliffs, New Jersey: Educational Technology Publications.

STOTT, John R. W. *Baptism and Fullness*. Downers Grove, Illinois: Inter Varsity Press, 1971.

THESE TIMES. "Guess Who Kids Look Up to Most." January, 1983.

TILLICH, Paul. *Dynamics of Faith*. New York: Harper and Brothers, 1957.

TILLICH, Paul. *The New Being*. New York: Charles Scribner's Sons, 1955.

TRAVIS, Robert. *Essentials of Learning*. New York: Macmillan Co., 1963.

UNGER, Merrill. *The Baptism of the Holy Spirit*. Chicago: Moody, 1974.

WAGNER, C. Peter. *Signs and Wonders Today*. Wheaton, Illinois: Christian Life Magazine, 1982.

WAGNER, C. Peter. *Your Spiritual Gifts*. Ventura, California: GL Publications, 1985.

WALVOORD, John F. *The Holy Spirit*. Grand Rapids: Zondervan Publishing Co. 1969.

WARFIELD, Benjamin B. *Miracles Yesterday and Today Real and Counterfeit*. Grand Rapids: William B. Eerdmans Publishing Co., 1964.

WESLEY'S Journal. Volume 1. Monday, January 1, 1739.

WILCKENS, Ulrich. "*Sopha*," in *Theological Dictionary of the New Testament*.

Printed in the United States
48980LVS00002B/475-522